# NO MIDDLE CLASS

## DISCOVER A NEW WAY OF LIVING

Foreword by Dr. John Avanzini

## ANDREW MERRITT

ISBN 13: 978-0-9637640-3-4

Bishop Merritt Ministries
www.bishopmerritt.org

# TABLE OF CONTENTS

# DEDICATION AND SPECIAL REMARKS

My wife, Viveca, and I, along with the Merritt family dedicate this book to the Straight Gate International Church family, past, present, and future.

To the servants of God and my fellow ministers of the Gospel, for our Father who has given to us the ministry of reconciliation through the preaching of the death, burial, and resurrection of Jesus; it is to you this book was written.

And finally, to all who read this book, the Holy Spirit is the Author and Revealer of scripture, and to this end, He has opened the scriptures to me within these pages. Not as a seed of controversy; but instead as a light of change and challenge to the Body of Christ and beyond.

As one unified Church we must stand on the Truth that is given to us in the Word of God, because He has given us all things that pertain to life and Godliness. Always remember this as a foundation of our faith.

*"Then God said, 'Let Us make man in Our image, according to Our likeness; **let them have dominion** over the fish of the sea, over the birds of the air, and over the cattle, **over all the earth** and over every creeping thing that creeps on the earth.'"* (Genesis 1:26 NKJV)

*"'The silver is Mine, and the gold is Mine,' says the LORD of hosts. 'The glory of this latter temple shall be greater than the former,' says the LORD of hosts. 'And in this place I will give peace,' says the LORD of hosts.'"* (Haggai 2:8 NKJV)


Yours in the Yoke of the Master,

Bishop Andrew J.D. Merritt

No Middle Class
# FOREWORD

I write this foreword from a unique prospective. I have always been an admirer of Bishop Andrew Merritt. Although it is only in the last decade that I have been in close proximity with him. However, for the past 40 years I have been speaking of the exceptional work, he has been doing. For not only was he teaching the Word and winning souls to the Lord. He was lifting his congregation as well as the neighborhoods surrounding his church, out of poverty and into prosperity.

Dr. Andrew Merritt pioneered whole community restoration, when the concept was still in its infancy. I describe Bishop Merritt as a soul winner, church builder, and economic evangelist. Bringing all those who follow him into upward mobility both spiritually and financially. Your time in this book will reveal powerful Biblical principles merged with common sense knowledge of everyday life.

Thank you, Sir, for showing us how to merge the Spiritual with the Practical.

Dr. John Avanzini

# No Middle Class
## PREFACE

The heart of God is lavish towards humanity. If you don't believe me? Just stop and look around you. Every day we walk through multiple varieties of gifts from the ground, air, and sea that He created with His family in mind. There is no way to miss His extravagant gestures of provision and piety towards us.

From the beginning He couldn't stop Himself from making sure that everything you needed, wanted, or desired was made available to you *before* you were created.

He knew that I would love pears, so He didn't stop at one type of pear; He made ten[1] for me to choose from. There are over sixteen types of lettuce[2] for salads lovers, and I just read an article that listed over 35 different eatable berries[3] that we consume in the United States regularly.

---

[1] https://usapears.org
[2] Watson, M. (2017, December 12) Lettuce Varieties, https://www.thespruceeats.com/varieties-of-lettuce-4065606
[3] https://www.gardeningchannel.com/list-of-types-of-berries/

I could go on and on with examples of the abundant provision from His bounty. But none of them would compare to the matchless gift of giving us—Himself. And He didn't do this just once, He did it twice!

*"And the Lord God formed man of the dust of the ground and breathed into his nostrils the breath of life; and man became a living being."* (Genesis 2:7 NKJV)

*"And as Moses lifted up the serpent in the wilderness, even so must the Son of Man be lifted up, that whoever believes in Him should not perish but have eternal life. For God so loved the world that He gave His only begotten Son, that whoever believes in Him should not perish but have everlasting life. For God did not send His Son into the world to condemn the world, but that the world through Him might be saved."* (John 3:14-17 NKJV)

When I started on the journey of writing this book, I had a clear agenda in mind. I wanted to rally people all over the world around the truth that God doesn't have a limit to His love, so there is no way that we should experience limitations in any other area of our lives either.

The boundless possibilities that are stored in the fabric of man are being displayed all over the world every day, but there is still something missing. And that's what this book was written to address.

The conversation in these pages is about unfolding the case that God didn't stop in the middle of His plan and leave us without hope. He gave us access to a life of true abundance in every sense of the word, but it can't be experienced apart of Him.

Yes, you can have all the money in the world, but lack the peace of mind to enjoy it, if you don't understand that all provision comes from God. Or you can be the poorest person on record, preparing to eat your last meal and die. But if you understand that there are principles to provision, you can eat like a king with a buffet of flavors to choose from.

However, if you and I lack the understanding of how we reached this point in the dispensation of time, there is no way that we can truly experience the limitless supply of God's blessing in this earth. I'm not talking about an occasional miracle when your back is against the wall. I'm talking about walking in the blessing of God that is poured out on your life like a fresh oil that never leaves and always abides.

*"You have made him to have dominion over the works of Your hands; you have put all things under his feet."* (Psalm 8:6 NKJV)

See, at the unveiling of creation, God gave Adam control over everything. I mean e-v-e-r-y-t-h-i-n-g!

Because He had created all things with Adam in mind. Nothing was off limits and everything was subject to Him. God had only made man a little lower than angels, so everything in earth was under Adam's' control—until.

Until he voluntarily surrendered it to satan. Then in an instant, sin entered the garden, and the man who had been given everything became subject to satan and the elements of nature that he had been created to control.

Listen to me, this is how the concept of 'survival mode'

entered the earth. Adam went from one extreme to another from thriving to surviving. He went from living in the blessing to learning how to function under the curse.

Which is what many people are doing even today. They are living under a cursed system that can't produce enough provision to sustain the demand of the people that depend on it.

That is until they do what Adam did and voluntarily surrender to one life over another. Only this time, leaving lack behind and embracing God's life and His way of doing things.

NO Middle Class is going to invite you into a real relationship with the One who owns everything. And I get the privilege of taking this journey along with you. Every verse has been a reminder of His faithfulness and each account has served to reignite the fire of my faith to see the blessing on my life produce even more revelation and favor than ever before.

Why? Because He is constantly giving of Himself to those who seek Him. You can't go hungry when you are attached to His Word. There is no way that you will fail, when you mind the things that please Him, following His commandments. You won't drown and you can't go under, because He is holding you up.

I pray that by the end of this book, you will have renewed or received the blessing of salvation in your heart. Where a cycle of peace and joy are running rampant in your soul. I am believing that the author of all scripture will be speaking to your heart about your family and your household. Giving you inside information on how to execute the principles of the Word of God, so that you will climb higher in every area of your life. Experiencing with great manifestations the declaration that we find in Haggai 2:8-9:

*"'The silver is Mine, and the gold is Mine,' says the Lord of hosts. 'The glory of this latter temple shall be greater than the former,' says the Lord of hosts. 'And in this place, I will give peace,' says the Lord of hosts."* (Haggai 2:9 NKJV)

My heart is that you be so open to the love of God and the fellowship of His Spirit that you see the blessing in full operation, not only in your life, but in your community, the nation, and the world.

Like the cloak of covenant, I want you to believe and receive the blessing of God. I'm referring to the Lord commanding, (*giving an authoritative order*) of the blessing on your life.

***"The Lord will command the blessing on you*** *in your* ***storehouses and in all to which you set your hand,*** *and He will bless you in the land which the Lord your God is giving you."* (Deuteronomy 28:8 NKJV)

And opening (*allowing access and passage of*) His good treasure over that of your household.

***"The Lord will open to you His good treasure,*** *the heavens, to give the rain to your land in its season, and* ***to bless all the work of your hand.*** *You shall lend to many nations, but you shall not borrow."* (Deuteronomy 28:12 NKJV)

Everything is possible and nothing is being held back. We have everything that we could ever need or want in Him. We don't have to stop in the middle of circumstances and hang out there. Neither should we adopt a mindset that there is a destination of how far God is willing to take us. The middle is a matter of mindset only if you allow it to be.

There is no middle class, because God doesn't have a ceiling that stops us from soaring. We are going to look at how the limitations of class can derail your creativity, currency, and call of God on your life.

Let's dive further into some controversial assumptions as I continue to unpack the assertion that the modern-day middle class is a myth that's loaded with lies and misleading the masses. But don't take my word for it, I want to show you what His Word says!

*"In the beginning was the Word, and the Word was with God, and the Word was God."* (John 1:1 NKJV)

Don't forget! We're doing this together and I'm declaring from the beginning, that in the heart of God, there is NO Middle Class!

## No Middle Class
## INTRODUCTION

There is no multiple choice—no middle ground—no grey areas. The middle class is a myth, thought up by the media, political pundits, and religious leaders to make room for mediocrity and indecision.

Have you accepted the lie that the height of your success stops somewhere in the middle enough times until you actually believe it?

My question is aimed to detect whether the brainwashing has worked. I'm not asking you if you close your eyes and say a prayer over your money each month. Nor am I asking if you have learned to work the system, and like a lotto machine, live off the spoils of others.

The dogma of the middle class was a devised plan of sociologists, economists, and a political ecosystem that strings along the carrot of contentment as a demonic replacement for the divine dominion that is available for *all* those who would believe.

But I've come to set the record straight!

There is NO Middle Class for the man or woman that has been redeemed from the reality of the curse of the law and all the restrictions that come with it. Simply by believing in their heart and confessing with their mouth, the complete rulership and authority of Jesus Christ and His outward demonstration of love so dominate and profound until time split to mark the occasion!

Today is the day that you drop the sustained satisfaction with living in survival mode behind!

I'm drawing a line of Life from the unfolding of creation to the crisis of classes, revealing the sinister saturation of lies about the heart of God and abundant life hovering in-between.

You are either born of the first Adam or reborn of the second who is Jesus Christ. Because He is Supreme, He cannot be a subordinate to anyone or anything. Abundant life is God's life.

It's as simple as that.

No one who is born-again can say that he or she is born of God and yet embrace a middle-class mindset. It's inconceivable to think that the same people who confess the redemption of the Cross would settle into what amounts to the cushy comfort of lack, limitations, and financial defeat.

*"The Lord will make you the head, not the tail. If you **pay attention to the commands of the Lord your God** that I gave*

*you this day and carefully follow them, you will always be on top, never at the bottom."* (Deuteronomy 28:13 NIV)

Embracing the mindset of the middle class is essentially refusing to give yourself fully to the commands of God. He promises to make you the head of every sphere of life, whether you are an accountant or a carpet cleaner.

Because it is in the heart and hand of God where the stage is set for you to experience the wealth of peace and provision that is available to those who seek to serve His agenda above that of their own.

*"But seek first his kingdom and his righteousness, and all these things will be given to you as well."* (Matthew 6:33 NIV)

Middle-class thinkers are always focused on monetizing their message before promoting His Gospel. There is nothing ventured and no expectation of advancement for people who are looking to hoard instead of harvest.

*"Therefore pray the Lord of the harvest to send out laborers into His harvest."* (Matthew 9:38 NKJV)

Your ceiling was destroyed when Jesus ascended out of the pit of hell with keys in His hand and death by the throat.

Don't live in a box any longer, with bars and begging surrounding you. Like the strings of a symphony, every ban was destroyed from your life through His death, burial, and resurrection.

The time has come to change your attitude and propel your momentum. But, that only happens as you surrender your thoughts from the erroneous view of an in-between God to one that has no limits of how far He will take you when your will is submitted to His plans.

There is freedom ahead of you through revelation and declaration. However, you must make the decision to be free. You don't have to live below 'see' level once the scales are removed from your eyes. I want you to see that you have been sold a bill of goods designed to hold you back.

I am determined to declare what others want to keep silent. It's the Word of God that is profitable and produces the **more** abundant life. You can take the Bible, study it, and cause wealth and richest to be in your house[4]. If you believe and apply what's contained therein. Because God's Word is the only thing that produces the more abundant life.

Forsake the folly of financial freedom laced in lack and surrounded by the limits that have plagued your life for far too long. It's time to leave the fight to assimilate into a system that simply does not display the heart of God behind. Raise your expectation beyond fiction and move into fact. Then watch God reveal what's available to the person that accepts the reality that there is NO Middle Class for those who discover a new way of living!

---

[4] Psalm 112:3

## Chapter One
### **Value Added**

As you journey through the pages of this book, the enemy will probably try to create fear or doubt in you. Don't let him affect you in any way. For the Bible says, *"I am the LORD your God. I am holding your hand, so **don't be afraid**. I am here to help you."* (Isaiah 41:13 CEV)

The revelation that you are about to receive is not new truth. It is neglected truth that has been previously overlooked by a lack of knowledge or religious tradition.

Whenever someone starts to discuss the improving or elevating of a person's standard of living—satan immediately moves in and starts with excuses and even fearfulness. It's old but effective because most people don't like getting out of their comfort zone!

Whether secular commentary or Biblical truth, people experience very strong emotions when it comes to their financial status, because in many ways their money represents their very lives.

*"So are the ways of every one that is greedy of gain; It taketh away the life of the owners thereof."* (Proverbs 1:19 ASV)

Your money is actually your life, because you spend length of days and hours of life to earn the money you have!

When a person discusses the financial well-being of your life; there is a natural tendency towards resistance and skepticism. People are reluctant to place their financial future into the hands of another.

That is, until someone brings to you the truth of the Word of God about how He really feels about you and your future. There is nothing to fear when it comes to God and your finances. As a matter of fact, this book will reveal to you how God uses a sufficiency of money to provide for your needs and desires. It is much higher so much higher, deeper, and fuller to God than just coins and currency.

As we follow the principles and precepts in His Word, you will see that the very area where you tend to eliminate God's involvement, is the place you will see the greatest demonstration of His love.

As we move forward, remember God is interested in every aspect of your life. For God declares, *"Even the hairs on your heads are counted. So **don't be afraid!** You are worth much more than many sparrows."* (Luke 12:7 CEV)

In this verse, Jesus gives a frame of reference for our immense value to Him. Money has value in the earth because we need it to live. It's our daily needs that gives it such prominence in our lives. But Jesus comes in and turns everything upside down. Showing us that real value lies in your position in the mind and heart of God.

His heart is seen in His Word, manifested in holiness, love, joy, blessing, and abundance. Now get ready for this, He says if you truly want to see something of supreme value to God, then look at yourself!

What could be more valuable than the exquisite human person He created you to be? And then He deposited His own life and righteousness into you. *"I am crucified with Christ: nevertheless I live; yet not I, but Christ liveth in me: and the life which I now live in the flesh I live by the faith of the Son of God, who loved me, and gave himself for me."* (Galatians 2:20 KJV)

There are some valuable automobiles, but you are more valuable than any automobile.

There are some valuable mansions, but you are more valuable than any mansion.

There are some valuable paintings, but you are more valuable than all the world's great paintings put together.

All the world's gold, silver, or rubies? You are still more valuable in God's eyes.

Nothing in the world is worth more than you! And that includes a large bank account and the sum of all the world's possessions.

Jesus didn't die on the cross to acquire earthly goods. He died on the cross to acquire people and glory to God, you are one of the ones He died for. As a by-product of His overwhelming gift of life, He also bestowed upon you the master key to acquire all the earthly things needed to operate as the royal ambassadors of the kingdom of God.

*"According as his divine power hath given unto us all things that pertain unto life and godliness, through the knowledge of him that hath called us to glory and virtue."* (2 Peter 1:3 KJV)

There is nothing to fear when you are a citizen of God's kingdom. You have the Creator of all things on the inside of you!

*"For you died, and your life is hidden with Christ in God."* (Colossians 3:3 NKJV)

There is nowhere for fear to operate once a person has wrapped their finite mind around God's infinite possibilities.

**Fear Is Not Your Portion**

Many people are in situations so plagued by fear that they cannot imagine a minute free from its control. If for some reason, you are that person, meditate Isaiah 41:13 and Luke 12:7 until you can only see the God who made heaven and earth ready to provide all you need and want for you.

*"I am the LORD your God. I am holding your hand, so **don't be afraid**. I am here to help you."* (Isaiah 41:13 CEV)

*"Even the hairs on your heads are counted. So **don't be afraid!** You are worth much more than many sparrows."* (Luke 12:7 CEV)

Take these two verses and place them around your house and on your mobile devices, your computers, and your refrigerator door so you can refer to them throughout the day.

Meditate on these verses by turning them over and over in your heart. Each time a thought comes that you won't become all that God says you be, confess them with your mouth. Drive out the satanic invasions that attempt to saddle you with the fear that for some reason, God doesn't have enough to provide for your every need and every godly desire.

Don't trade-in your lofty position in God for a mindset that would hold you hostage to limitations and self-defeat.

God has victory for you at every turn. He is right there making sure that His plan and purpose for your life comes to pass. When you function in fear it causes you unnecessary anxiety that stalls your progress while it weakens your faith.

**Don't Do It!**

Refuse to allow the hellish negative emotions and illusions of failure to stop you from excelling in this beautiful life that God has planned for you. Forget about anything that stopped you before. Ask God for His wisdom to move with a new understanding and anointing to move up into the life that God has for you.

*"Now to Him who is able to do exceedingly abundantly above all that we ask or think, according to the power that works in us."* (Ephesians 3:20 NKJV)

## Chapter Two
# Working with Averages

The power of God is <u>not</u> an average after thought that you and I can turn on and off like a light switch. Instead, it is a very potent and abiding power. This power functions both internally and externally, affecting every segment of your lives. However, this power doesn't just hunt you down and force Himself on you. This power only belongs to those who know how to accept Him and allow Him to work in their life.

As we journey through the scriptures together, you will gain a whole new perspective because you will see truth in the Word that will make this great power of God begin working in your own life.

Please note that this book doesn't come from my natural mind but that these are words that came to me directly from the heart of God. This message is about helping you not hurting you. Please let me share it with you with same passion and conviction that it came to me.

## Who Really Just Wants to Be Average?

When things are average, that really means that it neither hot nor cold, now how exciting is that? Think with me, how unexciting just average really is. For instance,

News Reporter: *"The DOW remained sluggish because XYZ company reports <u>average</u> earnings last quarter."*

Investment Strategist: *"Investors are nervous due to the reports of <u>average</u> sales during the holiday season this year."*

Financial Correspondent: *"ABC company will not be expanding its workforce because of <u>average</u> profits."*

People want to rise above average, you can see it in the urgency of concerned parents at report card time. Parents push their children to do better in school if they come home with an *average* grade.  People shy away from lackluster restaurant and dining establishments that are rated average because no one wants *average* food or service.

Even those who attend church don't want to hear an *average* sermon or have an *average* experience in the house of God. We all want to have better because were just created that way.

God is not average, He is exceptional, and He has hard-wired His creation to be just like Him!

*"Then God said, 'Let Us make man in Our own image, according to Our likeness: let them have dominion **over** the fish of the sea, **over** the birds of the air, and **over** the cattle, **over** all*

*the earth and **over** every creeping thing that creeps on the earth.'*

*So God created man in His own image; in the image of God created He created him; male and female He created them."* (Genesis 1:27-28 NKJV)

From the beginning, God created you to be **over** everything good He made. Does God's placement of man over the things He created sound like He envisioned mankind to be average?

**Absolutely not!**

Average people cannot command respect. They do not rule their environment. They settle for less than the best, and they sit with their hands in their lap praying to avoid the worst, jubilant that they can get by with tolerable outcomes. (Notice how the word 'tolerable' sounds so much like the word 'terrible'?)

Laziness oozes from the bones of those who settle with being just average. Because being the best requires the most.

- The most courage.
- The most work.
- The most responsibility.
- The most visibility.
- The most rejection.
- The most ridicule.
- The most misunderstanding.

- The most risk.
- The most setbacks.
- The most mistakes.
- The most tears.
- The most prayer.
- The most loneliness.
- The most work.

And yes, ultimately, the most reward.

Average people are destined to be ruled by those who are willing to pursue their God given positions of authority in Christ with passion. Like a baby sparrow waits for its mother to bring a worm. So is the man or woman who refuses to leave the comfort of average and step out and claim all the wonderful gifts and promises that God is so ready and willing to give them that will step out of their comfort zone and join Christ in the harness of His will for their lives.

*"Take My yoke upon you and learn from Me, for I am gentle and lowly in heart, and you will find rest for your souls. For My yoke is easy and My burden is light."* (Matthew 11:29-30 NKJV)

**What Are You Waiting For?**

*"1 After this there was a feast of the Jews, and Jesus went up to Jerusalem.*

*2 Now there is in Jerusalem by the Sheep Gate a pool, which is called in Hebrew, Bethesda, having five porches.*

*3 In these lay a great multitude of sick people, blind, lame, paralyzed, waiting for the moving of the water.*

*4 For an angel went down at a certain time into the pool and stirred up the water; then whoever stepped in first, after the stirring of the water, was made well of whatever disease he had.*

*5 Now a certain man was there who had an infirmity thirty-eight years.*

*6 When Jesus saw him lying there, and knew that he already had been in that condition a long time, He said to him, 'Do you want to be made well?'*

*7 The sick man answered Him, 'Sir, I have no man to put me into the pool when the water is stirred up; but while I am coming, another steps down before me.'*

*8 Jesus said to him, 'Rise, take up your bed and walk.'*

*9 And immediately the man was made well, took up his bed, and walked. And that day was the Sabbath."* (John 5: 1-9 NKJV)

Complacency is a killer. It will cause you to stay in a place of comfort for far too long.

The Webster 1828 Dictionary defines *complacence* as *"Pleasure; satisfaction; gratification. more than approbation, and less than delight or joy."* (Definition: Complacence, 2018)

When you find yourself stuck in the middle of life, between where you are and the place that you know that God wants to take you. Don't stop moving forward until you reach the top!

You aren't at the bottom, but you also aren't exerting any effort towards existing at the top—the place God designed for you.

He commanded you to have dominion. Dominance over anything that would hinder or stop you at any point from living in a place of authority on this earth. And for this man at the pool of Bethesda, we can see how easy it is to misinterpret where we are in relation to where God wants us to be.

From this encounter we can gather enough vital information to identify, alter, and move beyond complacency. Let's observe the text more closely.

In these nine verses there are vital keys that will serve you well as you ready for God's best.

*"Now there is in Jerusalem by the Sheep Gate a pool, which is called in Hebrew, Bethesda, having five porches."* (verse 2)

The porches in this verse are colonnades; long rows of columns usually covered by a roof. These were massive structures. Imagine how many sick people must have been crowded together on those porches. There could have been a multitude!

## KEY #1

### Just because complacency is expected doesn't mean it should be tolerated.

There will always be masses of complacent people around you. I'm sure if I asked you to write a list of all the people you know who are still sitting in the same place this year as they were last year, you wouldn't have any trouble with names coming to mind—including your own.

Our society tolerates laziness. It encourages people to just sit and wait for life to happen to them. The moment you give into living the status quo existence, the extinguisher of the greatness God has planned for you will try to lock you in a rut of indifference that is so difficult to rebound from.

Just like our scripture says, the sick used those porches as a habitual hiding place. Yes, these porches provided shelter from the elements, but above all it also provided an environment where shrinking back and making excuses was an acceptable way of life. It was a breeding place of complacency which was perfectly acceptable to all those around them.

**What are you hiding from?**

You might think that I'm being harsh here. But let's keep examining these verses because there are additional keys to discover, which will open our understanding further.

## Key #2

## Take a no excuses approach.

Not knowing when the water was going to be stirred, they simply sat complacent and waiting.

Jesus notices this man out of many that laid sick there. He approaches him and asks the man a 'yes or no' question, "Do you want to be made well?" But instead of addressing the question, he answers him with an excuse. An excuse which brings to mind the words found in Matthew 12:37 (NKJV):

*"For by your words you will be justified, and by your words you will be condemned."* (Matthew 12:37 NKJV)

Upon reading this passage, does it make you wonder why an excuse was the first thing that came out of the sick man's mouth? Is it because he had asked himself that same question a thousand times before and he simply repeats that which was already in his heart?

He must have already asked himself all the why's in the world:

- Why in the world am I sitting here?
- Why have I allowed myself to sit here this long?
- Why is the world against me?
- Why have I been forgotten?
- Why haven't I been picked?
- Why am I being ignored?
- Why hasn't anyone had pity on me?
- Why doesn't anyone reach out to me?

34

- Why doesn't anyone like me?
- Why am I cripple?
- Why did God make me like this?
- Why don't my legs work?
- Why can't I walk?
- Why am I still laying here?
- Why me? Why me? Why me?

Now notice how the sick man answers, *"Sir, I have no man to put me into the pool when the water is stirred up; but while I am coming, another steps down before me.'"* (verse 7)

In order to stop the noise of 'why,' he settled on the age old standby, "It's someone else's fault."

Then finally, silence. It worked. The propaganda he fed himself brought peace. He had come to the place where he was able to 'live' with his condition. Hope for change was almost all gone. Making the rumbling noises that he heard around him when the water was stirred tolerable. After all, he didn't have anyone to put him in the pool when the water was stirred.

This poor man had settled for average for he was sick and everyone around him was sick. So he was just average and learned to just live with it. That is until Jesus showed up.

Dr. Mike Murdock once made a statement that shifted my personal thoughts on tolerance. He said, *"What you can tolerate, you cannot change. You must hate the present to change it."*

Those sick people at the pool allowed the tolerance of their situation to anchor them in the false relief of being just average (better than the worst and worse than the best).

But God was going to use this man to shake the foundation of every person there, by taking a "No Excuses" approach to his complacency.

---

## Key #3

### You don't need what you think you need.

*"Jesus said to him, 'Rise, take up your bed and walk.' And immediately the man was made well, took up his bed, and walked. And that day was the Sabbath."* (verses 8-9)

At the end of verse 7, one might think that Jesus was going to have a conversation with the man about his illness. Maybe some of you were thinking that he would have engaged the man by asking him about his past or his upbringing.

Nope. Jesus did not come to discuss the man's problem. He came to change the man's reality to one that reflected the heart of the Father instead of the lie of satan. Jesus knew this man still had a desire for health and healing.

*"But Jesus did not commit Himself to them, because He knew all men, and had no need that anyone should testify of man, for He knew what was in man."* (John 2:24-25 NKJV)

Otherwise, He would not have been able to tell the man to pick up his bed and walk.

Jesus was challenging the man's faith. And even though this invalid must have asked himself, "Why?" a million times as we waited for help, just that was enough faith for Jesus to work with.

*"So Jesus said to them, 'Because of your unbelief; for assuredly, I say to you, if you have faith as a mustard seed, you will say to this mountain, "Move from here to there," and it will move; and nothing will be impossible for you.'"* (Matthew 17:20 NKJV)

So, instead of Jesus having a discussion with the man about his position of stagnation, by teaching him a faith message called, *"3 **Steps to Pick Up Your Bed**,"* He preached to him the most powerful seven-word message that would echo throughout eternity that day: *"Rise, take up your bed and walk."*

## Rise.

Get yourself up. Stop lying there wallowing in your own self-pity. Your living conditions do not reflect the dominion that God has placed in you.

The first thing that every person who is in complacency must do—you must rise. Remember, you decide whether you want to live as the head or the tail.

## Take Up Your Bed.

Don't leave that thing you have been lying on for someone else to scoot to and get comfortable. Jesus was blocking the spirit that allows people to become comfortable in their lowly state of excuses and self-pity.

Remember there were a lot of other sick people gathered at the pool that day. Had he told the man, "Rise and walk," without taking up his bed, the invitation for others to take his place would be too tempting for someone else to pass up.

Jesus was speaking to every sick person present who would believe. The man believed what he said so he rose up. But he didn't have to be the only one who stood.

Anyone that was in the sound of the voice of Jesus could have started moving their body to get up and have strength come to their muscles and bones. He cares for you as much as any other person past, present, or future.

I am convinced if the blind had started lifting their eyelids, their eyes would have come open. Multiple healing manifestations could have happened on those five porches that day. You don't believe this?

I can prove it to you.

*"... Because they have forsaken the Lord, the fountain of living waters."* (Jeremiah 17:13 NKJV)

Jesus never mentions the water of that stagnant pool because He is the water of life and healing. It was no longer about them getting to the water He was bringing the water to them!

*"Jesus said to her, 'Did I not say to you that if you would believe you would see the glory of God?'"* (John 11:40 NKJV)

Some of you have been waiting for things to happen at a certain time or in a specific way. I'm here to announce to you that <u>wherever Jesus is, breakthrough can be manifested in your life.</u>

Nobody had to wait on the angel anymore. Everyone there had access to the fountain of life. Water was ready to freely flow to everyone who would believe on Him. From the moment He said, "Rise," no one had any more excuses.

Once He speaks, you don't need permission to rise out of whatever situation you are in. Just obey the Word of the Lord and pull yourself up. Notice He didn't reach down and give him a hand up. It doesn't work that way. God is not going to lower His expectation to meet your situation. But He is always calling us to stand up to the image of God that He placed in us from the beginning (Genesis 1:27-28).

**Walk.**

Those porches became a platform. The Father's heart was manifested for everyone there to witness.

Jesus repeated what He'd heard the Father say. The Father said, *"Walk."* So, Jesus said, *"Walk."*

It's important to focus on this for a moment. Jesus could have told the lame man to simply stand and take up his bed. But what would that have done?

Once a cripple, the lame was now standing. Without listening and obeying the totality of the Word, he could have short-circuited the manifestation of the miracle. Not to mention, minimize the impact his testimony would have on other people.

The instruction to walk demonstrated that this wasn't a fluke. Walking engaged all the muscle groups—he was not just standing, he was walking. When the man, who was once lame, placed one foot in front of the other, the power of God was on full display.

The man's life suddenly turned from being an average crippled man into an outstanding testimony of what Jesus can do in any situation at any time for those who believe.

When you realize that you don't need the old familiar props that you once thought to be indispensable, your life will quickly turn around. That is when you begin to do those things the Word of God says you can do.

This man thought he needed an angel, stirred waters, someone to help him, a specific time on the calendar, and the approval of those at the pool. But none of that turned out to be the answer. **The only thing he needed was Jesus.**

The 'I AM' was standing in front of this man saying, "I AM everything you are ever going to need."

With Jesus, everything else becomes obsolete. Take hold of this truth today. With Jesus everything else becomes irrelevant. He is the only thing you need to steady yourself.

He is the One who commands angels. He is the fountain of living water. The One who moves beyond the limitations of time. The One that dispenses favor, and manifests miracles as you believe and acts on His Words.

It's Your Responsibility

Ultimately, Jesus was calling this man to responsibility. From the moment Jesus began to speak, He was motivating this man to respond to **His** ability that God had placed in Him.

Hear the question, *"Do you want to be made well?"* This was another way of asking, *"Do you want to take responsibility for your life?"*

Even the man's reply was about taking responsibility. *"Sir, I have no man to put me into the pool when the water is stirred up; but while I am coming, another steps down before me."*

He was saying, *"It's someone else's responsibility to help me get to the pool. I am incapable of taking care of myself."*

Now Jesus rectifies that forever by giving him the very thing he says he did not have. Making him, from that moment on, fully restored to a position of authority in the earth with the call of dominion over his own life.

*"Rise ..."* Now can you see why Jesus didn't bend down and give him a hand? It was no longer someone else's *responsibility* to pull him up. He had the strength, power, and faith to do it for himself.

*"... take up your bed ..."* That bed is in your charge now—not the other way around. Don't leave that bed there. Now that you have been healed,

> Once Jesus speaks, you don't need permission to walk out of your circumstance.

clean up after yourself. If you make a mess, then clean it up. That's your responsibility now.

*"... and walk."* Get moving. Be productive. It's time you go tell others about what I did for you. Not only that, but you have been surviving on the generosity of others for thirty-eight years. Now it's your time to go make a living.

Discover and use your gifts, talents, and abilities to generate income for yourself. It was time for this man to get to work.

*"For even when we were with you, we commanded you this: If anyone will not work, neither shall he eat. For we hear that there are some who walk among you in a disorderly manner, not working at all, but are busybodies."* (2 Thessalonians 3:10 NKJV)

Many of you have been healed, delivered, and set free from all manner of ungodliness. There's no time to sit around making excuses for not putting your hands to work doing something. Do you have a job? Do you volunteer in your community? Are you a dependable helper at your church? Are you productive in some area of society? Understand this, the Holy Spirit will manifest miracles for you when you decide to take responsibility for your life.

This is the way God works.

Jesus gave this man very clear instructions and it all came down to him taking his place as a productive citizen and effective witness for the Kingdom of God.

Maybe the reason this one lame man received his healing that day was because he was the only one that was ready to stand up and respond to the command of God to make use of the ability that was placed in him.

<u>He left the excuses behind.</u> He chose to live a life God could use to tell others about the day he picked up his bed and walked away from complacency.

The question is, are **you ready to do the same?**

## Chapter Three
## **Respond to Ability**

*"And God blessed them, and God said unto them, be <u>fruitful</u>, and <u>multiply</u>, and <u>replenish</u> the earth, and <u>subdue</u> it: and have <u>dominion</u> over the fish of the sea, and over the fowl of the air, and over every living thing that moveth upon the earth."* (Genesis 1:28 KJV)

In my estimation, one of the most powerful things God did was give man the assignment of caring for, and maintaining the earth. I have friends who are geologists and horticulturists who are truly passionate about the subject of God speaking to the earth and the earth still obeying His command some hundreds of thousands of years later.

*"As long as the earth endures, seedtime and harvest, cold and heat, summer and winter, day and night will never cease."*
(Genesis 8:22 NIV)

Guess what? The earth will never stop obeying God's voice. Just thinking about that makes me happy. But then a question comes to my mind:

Why don't people function the same way?

Or do we?

We saw in the previous chapter that Jesus healed a man and gave him the gift of once again being responsible for his own well-being in chapter two. But what was he truly responsible for exactly? Did he only have a responsibility to himself or was there a greater mandate that Jesus was giving the man at the pool of Bethesda when he instructed him to "*Walk.*" (John 5: 8 NKJV)

God's been giving man instructions from the beginning of time. The man and subsequently, the woman, were given their assignments on the earth. God made no good thing off limits for them to accomplish, *"... no good thing will he withhold from those who walk uprightly."* Psalm 84:11 NKJV So how did God do this? By giving them ability.

Isn't that essentially what Jesus gave the man at the pool when He was renewing his ABILITY.

He was now unlimited in his ABILITY to prosper and be in health. The man's body was now completely whole. He now had the ability to make choices, marry and support a wife and children. The ability to relocate to a more favorable job market. Everything was now new and open to him.

He was given the ABILITY to multiply his gifts and talents. He was no longer limited; his income potential immediately multiplied when he was healed.

The man now had the ABILITY to replenish! When he ran out of something and it needed to be filled, he didn't have to wait on someone else to fill it for him. He now had the ability to refill it himself.

He also had the ABILITY to subdue, or bring under control, or overcome, anything that would try to stop him from living and experiencing the fullness of God's provisions. Everything he lost when he lay on the ground had now come under his control physically, emotionally, and spiritually.

He had the ABILITY to dominate. <u>The dominion that was given in the garden was restored to his life because he had an encounter with Jesus.</u> He had not willed himself up from his sick bed. No, God had commanded him to get up. He had been restored to the place of authority that God intended for him from the beginning.

Understand this, our Lord Jesus is saying the same things to you and me today. You can place yourself in the scriptures, taking hold of the promises of God that restore any area of your life back to the full purpose that was in the Father's heart from the beginning. Jesus' death, burial, and bodily resurrection brought complete restoration of mankind—if you will believe in your heart and confess with your mouth.[5] It will be established to you.

"Rise!" is the first Word every person needs to hear when they are unemployed. It's the first Word every person needs to hear when they don't have proper or sufficient education.

---

[5] Romans 10:9-10

It's the first Word they need to hear in a hospital bed, when they are at the point of eviction, repossession, or bankruptcy.

Ultimately, the blessing of our life is that we have the ability to look after what God has given to us. This is still the mandate for every person today. We are to take what we have, no matter how small or insignificant it may seem, and perfect it and multiply it.

*"Then God blessed them, and God said to them, "Be fruitful and multiply; fill the earth and subdue it ..."* (Genesis 1:28 NKJV)

We can take dominion over our health, habits, and homes. It is up to us to activate **the ability** God has placed within you that will make the difference. Nothing more and nothing less.

The man at the pool of Bethesda responded to what Jesus said; meaning he responded to the Word of God.[6] Point blank. Period. **Every situation, whether financial or physical, starts and ends with your response to the Word of God.**

*"Now to Him who is able to do exceedingly abundantly above all that we ask or think, according to the power that works in us."* (Ephesians 3:20 NKJV)

The financial disasters and fallen economies around the world all stem from mankind departing from what God said.

---

[6] John 1:1

Even today, we see **families struggling financially not because of a lack of talent, but from a lack of response to God's Word.** Thereby stifling the ability, God has placed inside of them.

*"And the Lord God formed man of the dust of the ground and breathed into his nostrils the breath of life; and man became a living being."* (Genesis 2:7 NKJV)

One day I heard a woman at my church explain this verse to a group of school-aged children this way:

When you blow up a balloon, the air that is inside of you fills up the balloon so that it can fly. The balloon can't do anything until the air from inside of you is placed inside of it. Until someone blows into it, it just lies there unable to do what it was created to do.

The same is true for you and me. God blew into man and filled man up with His Spirit. So, whatever is in God is also in you. That's why any man or woman can rise from even the lowest financial state to a place of success and abundance. Don't let go of this because you have the life of God inside of you!

Even those who are not believers in Jesus Christ are working off the very sacred life that God placed in mankind. We cannot deny that the life of God is so potent that there are many who have done extraordinary things using only that first breath and blessing that God gave in the garden.

**Leave Disability Behind**

I'm going to say this again because we all need this deep in our spirits. You must leave the thoughts of disability behind. We just read that God has breathed into each of us His ability. In His ability, *all* things are possible literally. Meaning, we can do *all* things.

You might be saying, "Yes, but I have a physical limitation in my body." Sorry, but that's still no excuse. Just look at <u>Helen Keller, the first deaf-blind person to earn a Bachelor of Arts degree, graduating from Harvard University. She authored over 12 published books and several articles,</u>[7] without being able to see or hear.

This woman lost her sight and hearing as a child, but she didn't allow that to stop her from cultivating the abilities that God placed inside of her. With two of her senses gone, she was still able to be fruitful, multiply, replenish, subdue, and have dominion in her life.

She refused to allow the label "disabled" to become her reality and neither should you.

I know the government tells you that it's okay to sit around

---

[7] Wikipedia.com, Helen Keller (https://en.wikipedia.org/wiki/Helen_Keller)

in an unproductive mindset if you are disabled. The government will give you a check every month as long as you continue to live in your disability. How do I know? This is the way it goes with government assistance. Because I have personally seen it play out in my community and even in many churches.

I have seen people stand at the altar of God saying they are healed but would not go get a job. Why? Because they would lose the benefits for their disability. They get hurt and won't use their giftings because they are afraid if someone sees them cutting their grass then the government checks would stop rolling in.

I have even watched parents say they are believing for their child's healing but jump through hoops to make sure they can still receive a disability check for them. This is despite the fact that in many cases the child is still able to do all the things the disability check says they can't. These children have been labeled and are being used as a crutch, beyond that they are being trained for a life of dependence on the welfare system. *"Train up a child in the way he should go, and when he is old he will not depart from it."* (Proverbs 22:6 NKJV)

The moment you disengage from the ability that God has placed inside of you, the next logical step is to accept the limitations that pretending to be disabled brings to your life. Hence, your body will stay locked into what your mind tells it to whether you want it or not.

*"For as he thinks within himself, so he is. He says to you, 'Eat and drink!' But his heart is not with you."* (Proverbs 23:7 NASB)

On the power and authority of the Word of God that is vested in me, I am telling you to take up your bed and walk. Stop sitting there. For some of you that means you stop acting like you can't live without the disability check. There are people, children, and veterans who truly do have limitations until their healing manifests. However, a truly self-respecting Believer does not refuse to activate and operate the abilities that God has placed in them.

*"Now here is a command, dear brothers, given in the name of our Lord Jesus Christ by his authority: Stay away from any Christian who spends his days in laziness and does not follow the ideal of hard work we set up for you."* (2 Thessalonians 3:6 TLB)

There are always some folks that legitimately need financial assistance. However, let me caution those who are in this situation not to let government assistance become an addiction. If you find yourself in a difficult situation, there are three things that you can do immediately to change the trajectory of your life.

- Do you have a product or service idea that you can turn into a business?
- Is there a subject in school that you have always enjoyed or a hobby you would like to learn more about?

- Do you have a gift of encouraging others? Taking things apart? Singing? Writing?

Find that ability that God has placed in you that you can put into action right now to start turning your life into a dominating force for which you can only give credit to God.

The man at the pool couldn't give credit for those legs, that bed, or his journey to anyone but Jesus.

<u>Stop right now and have a conversation with the only One that matters.</u> Forget your friends who may or may not be in the system. Maybe no one else knows, but **God knows what's in you** and I suspect you also know what's in you.

## Are You Living Off Leftovers?

I have been a pastor long enough to know that asking a question like this could be the point where someone cues the music and a dance fest could start with just the tickling of a few keys in some churches.

Sadly, no one would ask what I consider to be the obvious question as an appropriate retort.

*"Whose leftovers are we talking about anyway?"*

Answer: Not yours.

Remember those people on those porches we talked about earlier? They were living off someone else's leftovers. Whatever was left over after their bills were paid. Whatever was left over after their vacation was taken. Whatever was left over after they paid for soccer practice, private school, gymnastics, or ballet.

That's a degrading way to live. But society primarily thinks about people living off leftovers when they pass a homeless person on the street. However, the truth is that there are millions of Americans who go to work every single day, pay their taxes, and even go to church that are living on the leftovers from someone else's table.

The Crisis of the Crumbs

*"But Jesus said to her, 'Let the children be filled first, for it is not good to take the children's bread and throw it to the little dogs.'*

*And she answered and said to Him, 'Yes, Lord, yet even the little dogs under the table eat from the children's crumbs.'"* (Mark 7:27-28 NKJV)

I know well-meaning people who are serving in the house of God. They may be preaching, teaching, pastoring, loving God with all their heart, yet they too are living off someone else's crumbs. Barely making ends meet. Having to ask for necessities because they haven't put into practice the principles that I am presenting to you throughout these pages.

Remember what I said about people focusing on what their household needs first? You see here that even Jesus reiterated this point.

*"But Jesus said to her, 'Let the children be filled first."*

Then He really pushes beyond theology and into a principle I think many people fail to see in these verses.

*"But Jesus said to her, 'Let the **children** be filled first, for it is not good to take **the children's bread** and throw it to the little dogs.'"*

Whose children is He referring to here?

HIS CHILDREN!

Are you seeing this! I know there are some that are not going to be able to handle what I say next. Maybe you should reread it again. Because in this verse, Jesus makes it clear that it's not proper for me to take from my family's needs and give to yours. It is my responsibility to make sure I have everything properly provided for in my household, before I tend to the needs of others.

> Sit down and have a seat. The table has been spread for you!

**Living from crisis to crisis or in need of an emergency financial miracle; this is not the will of God for your life.**

God has given you a dual role of 'servant' and 'supplier'. As a child of God, you are to serve those around you. But don't stop there, you are to serve yourself also. "But Pastor, why would you say serve yourself? That's not God's way."

Are you sure about that?

Jesus said, *"And you shall love the Lord your God with all your heart, with all your soul, with all your mind, and with all your* *strength.' This is the first commandment. And the second, like it, is this: 'You shall love your neighbor as yourself.' <u>There is no other commandment greater than these.</u>"* (Mark 12:30-32 NKJV)

There is no other commandment greater than loving God first and then loving yourself and your neighbor equally.

*"... Love your neighbor as yourself."* (verse 31)

"As" means *"equally; to the same degree, amount or extent."*

You cannot properly serve your neighbor unless you have first experienced a clear and precise demonstration of God's love for you.

God is saying, *"Love me with all you have, and I will love you with all I have. Then duplicate the love I have shown you with your neighbor."*

"Preacher what does this have to do with living off someone else?" I'm glad you asked.

In that love exchange with God, He is always going to lavishly love you. He is never, ever, going to see you without the things you need.

As a father properly takes care of His children, He is going to take care of you and your needs. And He will do it in a way that you won't ever have to depend on what someone has leftover to give you.

In the love relationship with the Father, He will start igniting ideas, witty inventions, supernatural creativity, and previously unrealized opportunities. Things that you never even dared to dream possible. In every one of these bursts of creativity, God will bring you into more and more opportunities for your peace, joy, and financial increase.

In fact, **you are never a leftover thought to God.** His thoughts toward you are those of peace and not of evil, to give you a future and a hope.

*"For I know the plans I have for you, says the Lord. They are plans for good and not for evil, to give you a future and a hope."* (Jeremiah 29:11 TLB)

He is thinking about your future all the time. There isn't a moment when He is not thinking about you. He knows everything from the smallest detail to the largest challenge that you face.

Remember, there are no leftovers with God because He makes everything new, from scratch every single day. (From scratch means fresh, new ingredients every day.)

*"Give us this day our daily bread."* (Matthew 6:11 NKJV)

God doesn't want you to have to eat day-old bread. You can ask the children of Israel. He provided new, fresh baked manna every single day. Truly, *He is new every morning.*

If you are living off the leftovers of others. It's not God's fault. Yes, the deck may be stacked against you, but you, yes **you** bear some of the blame. It's up to you to start doing something about the problem. You must seek God and find out where you got off track and get back in step with His opinion of you. I can't do that for you. Your family and friends can't do that for you. The government can't do that for you. You must go to the Father through the door of His Son, Jesus, to get your needs met. There is no other way around it.

If you are a pastor experiencing financial hardship and you don't understand why or how to get out from under it. I encourage you to seek God. Maybe there is something He has urged you to do in the past, but you have neglected to obey Him.

I am not being harsh; I am trying to help break you out of your problem. God wants success for you and I'm telling you it's attainable.

It could be that He is saying for you to wait on a project. Maybe now is not the time. It could be that He wants to pay for it out of His pocket instead of out of your budget.

Believe me, <u>there is no project that He is asking you to undertake that He will not finance.</u> Sometimes victory only comes when we get on His timetable. There are instances when it's the direction we are trying to go. Other times it is simply a case of disobedience to His instructions. From time to time, all of us have to remember <u>it is His kingdom to build and our assignment to obey.</u>

God is not limited in the ways He has to provide for you. It would be impossible to list the many ways and times that God has surprised me throughout my ministry. However, everything God has ever done has come down to my obedience to Him. I had to rely on His direction and an absolute belief in His Word. <u>God never created me to live off the leftovers from someone else's table.</u> He always had something better for me than I could have ever manifested for myself.

## Cooperation is Key

*"If you obey the Lord, you won't go hungry ..."*
(Proverbs 10:3 CEV)

It's a documented fact that God is going to make sure you are taken care of if you walk in obedience to His plan for your life. In my book, *The Word According to IF*, I explore the topic of conditions. While we pitter-patter through life, free from responsibility and an obligation to fulfill His agenda, do we really believe we can live life thinking that God really doesn't require anything from us?

The key to overcoming and living the 'good life' on this earth begins and ends with being WILLING AND OBEDIENT.

*"If you are willing and obedient, you shall eat the good of the land."* (Isaiah 1:19 NKJV)

God invites us to become a cooperative participant in His plan. Let's open our eyes to the fact that this is what separates the winners from the losers. The idle from the industrious. The willing from the weak.

Think about it.

Those who drive the best company cars are the ones who are doing the most work, dedicating themselves completely to diligently seeking the advancement of the company they represent. It's the CEOs who work long hours, make the hard decisions, use their ingenuity, and sacrifice their life for the company. These are the ones who command the highest salaries and receive the best benefits.

The more they put their abilities to use for the corporate agenda—the more valuable they become to that company, and the success they see with their company, the more success they see in their own lives.

One of the mighty men of valor at my church was talking to me about how sometimes blue-collar and white-collar workers don't understand the mindset of the other because typically, their experiences are very different. Both give themselves with great dedication to their professions, working long hours, sacrificing time with their families, and aspiring to a rise in wages and the benefits that come with their chosen professions.

Thus, white-collar workers expect to rise to the level of management where a company vehicle is part of the benefits package, whereas a blue-collar worker's expectation in their next level of output is a higher hourly wage. Neither is a right or wrong scenario. It simply comes down to what kind of work ethic they have been trained up with. A poor work ethic brings forth low accomplishment. While a good work ethic brings about great accomplishment and reward in whatever place they are in.

God has a much better way for climbing the ladder of success in life.

Believe me, He takes into consideration your output. But He rewards not solely based on position or title. Instead, it is greatly based on obedience.

Whether you build car parts, or hold the position as chairman of the board, as long as you are doing with great fervor the assignment for which God called you, with willingness, diligence, passion, respect, and love, you can expect that the goodness of God will see you rewarded in every aspect of your life. The same expectation of the goodness of God can be wonderfully experienced.

One of the primary keys is obedience. In other words, you must be committed to God's opinion and be in agreement with it. When your heart, mind, and actions shift from obedience to God; then everything about your life will begin to shift. Believe me, it has happened to me.

I've had to realign myself many times in life. It comes with the territory. I have been guilty of having good ideas that weren't God ideas and sometimes, I've fouled things up. But the essence of my heart has always been to be pleasing to God. Therefore, I correct my thinking back to God's way and as soon as I do, the mess that was unfolding would find solutions that would bring victory back to me and the people God has given me.

Being uncompromisingly committed to the operations of the Kingdom of God is the thing that has made the difference for me. I seek the will of the Chairman of the Board, who by the way is always Jesus. I want to be steered by Him in the way He wants me to go.

I must remember that <u>the answer to my success stems solely from my faithful execution of my assignment in His agenda.</u>

It's the submitted servant who will be allowed to rise in the ranks of the Kingdom of God. It won't be celebrities and show-offs. It's the submitted servant that warrants the spotlight.

## Mixed Messages

Beware of mixing the messages because you are traveling in two kingdoms. If you are a believer in Jesus Christ, your citizenship and allegiance to the kingdom of God must be the determining factor of your behavior here on earth. No matter how blurry the lines become, your provision doesn't come from the country you're visiting, it comes from the place of your real citizenship. Always remember, the child of God has his or her citizenship in heaven.

*"Consequently, you are no longer foreigners and strangers, but fellow citizens with God's people and also members of his household, built on the foundation of the apostles and prophets, with Christ Jesus himself as the chief cornerstone."* (Ephesians 2:19-20 NIV)

Everything about your life is tied to your faithful execution of your assignment in God's Kingdom. Nothing else really matters, whether you find yourself like Joseph of old in the comfort of a palace, the punishment of a prison, or the penalty of a pit.

## Chapter Four
## The Persecution of Poverty

*"**Wise people store up knowledge,** but the mouth of the foolish is near destruction.*

*The rich man's wealth is his strong city; **the destruction of the poor is their poverty.***

***The labor of the righteous leads to life,** the wages of the wicked to sin."* (Proverbs 10:14-16 NKJV)

Recently I heard a story about a lady who is going through some severe financial challenges. She is faithful in her church, loves the Lord, and has taught her children the ways of God for many years. However, by way of observation I know that this woman is always in the same cycle of poverty.

From one year to another the same situation keeps occurring. This poor woman's situation caught my attention because she claimed that it was God who was persecuting her. But that's not all.

She truly believes the longevity of her financial woes has something to do with God—not to do with herself.

Granted, she was definitely being persecuted, experiencing persistent hostility and harassment, but it surely wasn't coming from God. <u>The origin of her miserable existence was the result of her poverty.</u> And, like it or not, her problem was not the fault of satan, it was of her own doing.

The spirit of poverty had been given a place and she was completely ignorant of the fact that she in the power of God could have evicted that spirit from her life a long time ago. By simply using one God-given talent, she could have very possibly become a millionaire by now.

Yes, she had been serving with great diligence in her church. But if only she had used this same diligence to defeat the spirit of poverty that had been robbing her all these many years? She would have been set free many years before.

Living under the tyranny of lack leaves people with great shame and a sense of victimization. But that is not what God has intended for His people. I have said it before and I will say it again. <u>God has given you the power, strength, and ability to live on top of the world, not on the bottom.</u>

*"And the Lord will make you the head and not the tail; you shall be above only, and not be beneath, if you heed the commandments of the Lord your God, which I command you today, and are careful to observe them."*
(Deuteronomy 28:13 NKJV)

Instead of being crumb snatchers, you were destined to be bread makers. However, it is your responsibility to store up God's knowledge and then us it to supernaturally supersede the knowledge of man.

My question as I thought about this woman was "Why hadn't she gained enough information about starting a cleaning company to make everyone else's house as clean as hers?" (Because it was well known that her house was always spotless, floors so clean that you could eat off of them.)

It was mind boggling to me.

Why was she getting food assistance? Instead, she could have gone and purchased a couple buckets, sponges, rags, and her favorite cleaning solution, and called up a few friends to let them know she was taking appointments to clean houses.

I guarantee you she would have made more money doing that than the silly stipend of slavery the government had been providing her all these years.

I believe had she gone to her pastor with her idea, asked him to come into agreement about her business, made herself available to clean the church once a week, exercising Matthew 6:33, *"But seek first the kingdom of God and His righteousness, and all these things shall be added to you,"* and brought the first fruits of her increase (the profit from the first house she cleaned), she would have unlocked a flood of financial release like none that she had ever seen.

NO Middle Class: Discover a New Way of Living

*"¹ A certain woman of the wives of the sons of the prophets cried out to Elisha, saying, 'Your servant my husband is dead, and you know that your servant feared the Lord. And the creditor is coming to take my two sons to be his slaves.'*

*² So Elisha said to her, 'What shall I do for you? Tell me, what do you have in the house?' And she said, 'Your maidservant has nothing in the house but a jar of oil.'*

*³ Then he said, 'Go, borrow vessels from everywhere, from all your neighbors—empty vessels; do not gather just a few. ⁴ And when you have come in, you shall shut the door behind you and your sons; then pour it into all those vessels, and set aside the full ones.'*

*⁵ So she went from him and shut the door behind her and her sons, who brought the vessels to her; and she poured it out. ⁶ Now it came to pass, when the vessels were full, that she said to her son, 'Bring me another vessel.'*

*And he said to her, 'There is not another vessel.' So the oil ceased. ⁷ Then she came and told the man of God. And he said, 'Go, sell the oil and pay your debt; and you and your sons live on the rest.'"* (2 Kings 4:1-7 NKJV)

I've taught 2 Kings 4:1-7 for many years because it is a picture of how lack in financial matters makes us slaves to society, satan, and others. It leaves people vulnerable to the abuse and mistreatment of others. It strips people of the power God intended for them to operate in.

*"A certain woman of the wives of the sons of the prophets cried out to Elisha, saying, 'Your servant my husband is dead, and you know that your servant feared the Lord. And the creditor is coming to take my two sons to be his slaves.'"* (2 Kings 4:1 NKJV)

The widow in the book of 2 Kings was about to lose her sons to slavery. Can you imagine that? Her husband had served God and obviously she was also one who believed, because she went to the prophet to get his instruction.

Allow me to pause here for a moment.

Satan has done a job on the minds of people, including believers in Jesus Christ, with the obscure notion that they don't need a pastor or access to the prophet of God. That is simply not true.

If you are looking for a perfect pastor, let me stop you there—none exist. But there are people who truly have the heart of God and understand the call of service to the people that He sends to them.

Don't allow the delusion of perfection to alienate you from the blessing of having a pastor—one that regularly puts the Word of God out for all to hear. Everyone needs the Word that God regularly speaks to them. Everyone needs a man or woman of God to counsel with. Everyone needs a pastor ... period.

So, the widow woman goes for instruction and that is what she receives.

*"So Elisha said to her, 'What shall I do for you? Tell me, what do you have in the house?' And she said, 'Your maidservant has nothing in the house but a jar of oil.'*

*Then he said, '**Go, borrow vessels from everywhere**, from all your neighbors—empty vessels; do not gather just a few. And when you have come in, you shall shut the door behind you and your sons; then pour it into all those vessels and set aside the full ones.'"* (2 Kings 4:2-4 NKJV)

Elisha was directing this woman to where her financial miracle was located. It was in her house!

Immediately, I began to think about the woman with the spotless home. What she needed to break the cycle of lack off her life was located where? Her witty invention was in her house!

Can you see it?

The very thing that was going to generate an endless supply of revenue for this widow woman was the exact same thing for the woman in our illustration and her children.

> What do you have in your house?

The widow in the Bible had oil.

The single mother of our illustration has Windex®!

*"So she went from him and shut the door behind her and her sons, who brought the vessels to her; and she poured it out. Now it came to pass, when the vessels were full, that she said to her son, 'Bring me another vessel.' And he said to her, 'There is not another vessel.' So the oil ceased."* (2 Kings 4:5-6 NKJV)

This woman followed the instructions given to her.

She didn't make up her own rules as she went. Nope. She couldn't afford to get this wrong. There was too much at stake. Her babies' lives were hung in the balance. This was about much more than her and her sons, it was about her children and grandchildren too.

So she did then, what many people refuse to do today, and lifted the limitations off her life with a listening ear and a lot of **labor.**

## Let the Labor Begin

*"Then she came and told the man of God. And he said, 'Go, sell the oil and pay your debt; and you and your sons live on the rest.'"* (2 Kings 4:7 NKJV)

Today there is a disconnect between what is possible and what is pliable. You see the fairy tale that millionaires are made by sitting on the couch is a lie.

It's inconceivable to me that there is a segment of our society that has somehow told people they can be overnight wonders and amass great sums of wealth without putting forth their hands to do or produce something.

*"The Lord will command the blessing on you in your storehouses and in all to which **you <u>set</u> your hand**, and He will bless you in the land which the Lord your God is giving you.*

*The Lord will open to you His good treasure, the heavens, to give the rain to your land in its season, and **to bless all the <u>work</u> of your hand**. You shall lend to many nations, but you shall not borrow."* (Deuteronomy 28:8 &12 NKJV)

It is outrageous to think that God is going to give you an instruction to sit and wait on an answer for provision without it requiring your participation. Even the man at the pool of Bethesda had to rise. Jesus, the Living water was standing there stirring right in front of him. But Jesus didn't say, "Keep sitting there, I'm going to send your healing." No, the healing was activated the moment the man started lifting himself up.

The single mother could activate her financial miracle if she would pick up the phone, follow the example of the widow woman, and start asking her neighbors if they needed their house cleaned.

Who knows, there may be people who would jump for the chance to get her to clean their house. Maybe some had heard of her cleaning talent.

The widow woman's financial miracle was activated, and the oil released, the moment she asked for that first pot.

Many of you sitting there reading or listening to this book are ripe to experience a manifestation of God's Word right where you are.

At this moment, you are storing up knowledge that will facilitate the overcoming destruction of poverty. And when you put your hands toward that labor by faith, you are putting action to the Word of God in your life—which always produces favorable results.

*"**Wise people store up knowledge,** but the mouth of the foolish is near destruction. The rich man's wealth is his strong city; **the destruction of the poor is their poverty. The labor of the righteous leads to life,** the wages of the wicked to sin."* (Proverbs 10:14-16 NKJV)

You can destroy the potential you have by foolishness and exposure to poverty. Both stem from mental and spiritual deficiencies. You see it's not about money, it's about the mindset.

*"For as he thinks in his heart, so is he."* (Proverbs 23:7 NKJV)

There is something much worse than being poor. It's having a poverty mindset.

These women experienced completely different outcomes because of how they viewed what they had around them. Certainly, one of the key elements that separated their success was that one was willing to labor, and the other was not.

In general, I have found over these many years that this is a reoccurring theme for many people in society. This brings me to a subject that angers the poor and incites riots from the rich. It's the elephant in the room that separates people, classes, and bank accounts.

I'm talking about the lure of the lazy.

Lazy people leave their life behind in little spurts of solace that can't fill a cup. The Book of Proverbs is full of examples that the lazy offer nothing, produce nothing, and usually expect even less.

I recommend you do as I do which is spend my time with those who have sweat on their brow and fire in their eyes. <u>They are determined, dangerous foes to mediocrity, and enemies of anything average.</u> They know how to encourage themselves in a fight. They aren't weak, even if they may be small. They get the job done and stay true to the fight.

They have kissed the lure of laziness goodbye, choosing rather to pursue productivity that makes angels cheer and Heaven rejoice.

Simply put, the time has come for you to leave lack and laziness behind.

## Chapter Five
# The Lure of the Lazy

L aziness is an enticing luxury that bottom feeders cling to like a life preserver—latching themselves to wishes rather than work.

*"The soul of a lazy man desires and has nothing; but the soul of the diligent shall be made rich."* (Proverbs 13:4)

Did you notice this verse says, *"the soul of a lazy man?"* The soul is where the will, desires, and emotions are housed. Because of this, lazy people make decisions based on how they feel. If they don't feel like getting work done, they don't. It's an act of their will. They will themselves to do, or not to do, based on their fleeting desires at the time.

There is no way you can be head of anything, making decisions, taking actions, only when you feel like it. More often than not, you will not feel like doing the greater part of the things that must be done in accomplishing the will of God for your life.

*"For it is God who works in your both to will and to do of His own good pleasure."* (Philippians 2:13 NKJV)

God knows that His work in you is not complete by just igniting your will; but He also ignites your hands *"to do the things that please Him,"* what His good pleasure is in the earth.

The 'lacking lazy' is what I like to call them. Never maturing to a place of forward motion and movement. They refuse to make the effort to create opportunities for themselves and then putting them to work.

They make little or no contribution to their own lives, hanging out and waiting for something to happen for them. Rather than employing at the very least a workman's mentality that produces even the minimal required for them to live on, they choose to do little if anything.

I have found it unproductive to waste my time with lazy people. I have too much to do for God. Ultimately, just like them, I must answer to Him for the resource of time and talent that He has given me.

When I first started out as a pastor, I would counsel, beg, pray for, dance in a circle, cry, etc., trying to get people to engage in their own lives. Eventually, I grew up. I stopped the madness. Thus, allowing people the opportunity to follow or not follow the plan of God for their lives. We all must make our own decisions.

I stepped back and let them use both their will and actions to produce their own good work. Once I understood that a man's will is a gift, I have no right to take it from him, I was able to love, pray, and support those who wanted to move in the direction of faith that God was placing in my heart for our ministry and the wonderful people that God was sending me.

## Living Hand to Mouth

Satan is the only one who wants you to live hand-to-mouth. AND he is the only one who wants you to live in a lazy, lackadaisical, low-expectancy mindset. No one else wants that for you. However, you must realize that those around you don't have the power to stop the cycle you find yourself in. This cannot happen until you make the decision to change.

Sadly, I realize by the Spirit of God that most lazy people don't even realize they are wearing a cloak of laziness, with its many facets of indecision and regret.

*"A lazy man buries his hand in the bowl and will not so much as bring it to his mouth again."* (Proverbs 19:24 NKJV)

Every time I read this verse I chuckle inside. Now this is a pretty lazy fellow here. Can you imagine someone so lazy that he put his hand in a bowl and won't use his strength to even bring his hand back to his mouth.

Now that's LAZY!

However, when you are able to get beyond the physical, part of you, there are infinite spiritual implications locked inside the real you. The 'you' that God chooses to see.

*"... buries his hand ..."*

A lazy person buries the hands in idle trivia instead of using them to build a life worth living. God designed you to work with your hands. Buried hands or idle hands are hidden and inactive, unable or unwilling to produce anything worthwhile. If your hand is buried, then your earning potential is lying dormant as well.

Remember the master's servant in Matthew?

*"Then he who had received the **one talent** came and said, 'Lord, I knew you to be a hard man, reaping where you have not sown, and gathering where you have not scattered seed. **And I was afraid** and **went and hid your talent in the ground**. Look, there you have what is yours.'*

*But his lord answered and said to him, '**You wicked and lazy servant**, you knew that I reap where I have not sown, and gather where I have not scattered seed. So you ought to have **deposited my money with the bankers**, and at my **coming I would have received back my own with interest**. So **take the talent from him**, and give it to him who has ten talents.*

*For to **everyone who has, more will be given, <u>and</u> he will have abundance**; but from him who does not have, even what he has will be taken away. And cast the unprofitable servant into the*

78

*outer darkness. There will be weeping and gnashing of teeth.'"* (Matthew 25: 24-30 NKJV)

We know that the servant with the one talent didn't have a lot of ability. For earlier in this chapter of Matthew verse fifteen says that the servants received measures of money in relation to their ability. Because of this we know that this man had limited ability because he received the least money. This also means that his level of responsibility was not as great as the others with more ability.

*"But he who did not know, yet committed things deserving of stripes, shall be beaten with few. For everyone to whom much is given, from him much will be required; and to whom much has been committed, of him they will ask the more."* (Luke 12:48 NKJV)

And yet, by his own confession; he was afraid to trust God and just step out and attempt to multiply the one talent that had been put in his trust.

Let me make this very clear: Everything you have belongs to God. That is why this part of the Biblical account stands out to me. It wasn't his talent in the first place. It was his master's. Which is what God is doing with us today.

There is not one gift or ability you have that was not engineered into the overall plan of God for you since the beginning of your creation.

*"Before I formed you in the womb I knew[8] you, before you were born I set you apart; I appointed you as a prophet to the nations."* (Jeremiah 1:5 NIV)

For Jeremiah, he was appointed to be a prophet. For you it could be that God has appointed you to be a teacher, a physician, a coach, a business owner, or an engineer.

Listen, whatever it is that God has designed for you to be or do, you need to be aware constantly, that it is His design and His desire for your life that is important.

Lazy.

Even minimal effort will produce some increase. God is not saying that you must produce at the same rate as everyone else. Some just don't have the ability of others. But what is required of all is to do the best we possibly can with whatever God has entrusted you.

A lazy man or woman doesn't even exert the energy to think of even an easy way to be productive. This appears to have been the thinking of this slothful servant. Had he thought about even the simplest way to generate increase even if it had been with the least amount of effort, God could have smiled on him. Jesus shows that to be true by saying, "Hey, you could have simply made a bank deposit. At least I would have made some interest."

Don't get swept into the lie that God is not looking for an increase of His investment in you. That is a lie that satan

---

[8] Or chose

has been peddling from the beginning. The Father invested the life of His son, Jesus and expected an increase to come from the new life you have in Him!

What did God really want the life of Jesus to produce? That you would have a new life full of abundance.

*"... I have come that they may have life, and that they may have it more abundantly."* (John 10:10 NKJV)

You are no exception. As a matter of fact, you are a very important part of His expected increase.

Money gravitates to those who do not bury their God-given abilities. If you are born again, you are designed to be active in mind and productivity. That is what is meant in Matthew 13:12, *"For whoever has, to him more will be given, and he will have abundance; but whoever does not have, even what he has will be taken away from him."* With each ability that you use and develop, God will release more abilities. As this process develops in you, this develops a cycle of increase and development that health, wealth, and ample abundance in every aspect of your life.

Jesus left on record, how to generate abundance. Therefore, anyone who faithfully employs these principles will see increase in their lives.

A few principles are:

- Talents are not buried.
- Fear is not tolerated.
- Excuses are not made.

- Laziness is not allowed.

## Is Your Bowl Empty?

*"... his hand in the bowl ..."*

One of the reasons I chuckle at the verse in Proverbs about the lazy man who is face down in a bowl of oatmeal is because I always wonder, why did he place his hand in the bowl? If he is that lazy, what was he expecting to get out from the bowl?

He didn't put anything in ... so what was he going to pull out?

*"For even when we were with you, **we commanded you this: If anyone will not work, neither shall he eat.**"*
(2 Thessalonians 3:10 NKJV)

There was a time that parents reinforced this scripture from the moment a male child was born. By the time a little guy was 7 or 8 years old, he was begging for a paper route or to mow the grass. Why? Because he understood even at an elementary school level, that he had to produce something in order for his needs to be met.

Of course, at 7 or 8 in my generation, his need was for a baseball glove or baseball card. Now it could be a video game or new wireless gaming controller. Either way, the moment parents stopped reinforcing this scripture in their homes, you began seeing more boys hanging on the street corners and getting involved in all manner of mischief.

Why? Because God created us to be productive and active. He instructed that the moment Adam and Eve were placed in the garden, they were to tend to it (work). Every man should have a work ethic before he has anything else.

Before my daughters in the ministry get married, I sit down with their proposed husband to ask some very specific questions. One of the first questions I ask is, "Do you have a job?"

I don't fluff around with it, because a man who is not productive and responsible with feeding and taking care of himself, is not going to be responsible when it comes to taking care of my spiritual daughters either. And all of them will tell you that I don't sign off on unions like that.

Why do I take such a firm stance on this? Because how can a man take a wife with an empty bowl in his hand? He shouldn't be allowed to do this, but sadly, many do.

An empty bowl is a sign of a misguided life.

For instance, debt usually indicates a lack of understanding, a lack of discipline, or unwise decision-making.

For example, there is nothing wrong with having a credit card. The problem comes when the credit card is maxed to the limit, with no way of paying the balance.

I don't use this example to bring condemnation but illumination. Focus on being diligent in every area of your life and it will reveal order, not the messiness of disorder.

Lazy people don't live on top and empty bowls seldom, if ever end up in heaven.

*"Now when he had taken the scroll, the four living creatures and the twenty-four elders fell down before the Lamb, each having a harp, and **golden bowls full of incense, which are the prayers of the saints.**"* (Revelation 5:8 NKJV)

You don't see God keeping bowls without anything in them. And you should refuse to have bowls with nothing in them in your life as well.

Use your talents, gifts, abilities, prayers, and passions to produce something you can use to keep your life full of reproductive stewardship. Then God can honor you as an active participant in His will.

Honor Him today, by refusing to allow the lure of laziness to latch hold of you and the ones you love. God has great expectations, plans, and joys for your life. But only you can lie down and refuse to work your faith and labor with your hands to produce oracles of abundance in every category of your life.

There is no middle category of living for all those who understand that everything they have, are, and own was given to them as a full gift from God, not the deficient promise of man.

## Chapter Six
## **Leverage the Little**

*"And He looked up and saw the rich putting their gifts into the treasury, He saw also a certain poor widow putting in two mites.*

*So He said, 'Truly I say to you that this poor widow has put in more than all; for all these out of their abundance have put in offerings for God, but she out of her poverty put in all the livelihood that she had.'"* (Luke 21:1-4 NKJV)

When I consider the servant who was given one talent to manage, it stirs another thought in my heart. I know there must be some people reading this book who feel as though they have nothing to offer to God or anyone else for that matter.

So let me encourage you with this truth: EVERYONE has something to contribute to the world.

God is faithful in that regard. He doesn't create an expectation without giving you what you need to fulfill it. Ironically, that removes all the excuses most people make about not being able to reach higher, accomplish more, and live productively throughout their life.

Say what you will. God has placed something in everyone to bring glory to His kingdom and resources to their life. Then why are there so many people who have settled into a menial lifestyle?

Because they haven't learned to leverage the little.

Out of everything I have written in this book thus far, this practical concept is one of the most important. People who are successful in the affairs of life have learned to operate the concept of leverage.

In the simplest terms, **leverage** is *using something to its maximum advantage*. I believe many of you are losing out on tremendous avenues for wealth and financial increase for your homes and families, because you have not mastered the proficiency of leverage in your everyday affairs.

Leveraging is laced into every fabric of this earth. But it is not a concept that has been conceived by men. We see leverage from the beginning. Even before He formed Adam and extracted Eve, God incorporated leverage in the ecosystem of life.

*"In the beginning God created the heavens and the earth. The earth was without form, and void; and darkness was on the face of the deep. And the Spirit of God was hovering over the face of the waters. Then God said, 'Let there be light;' and there was light."* (Genesis 1:1-3 NKJV)

What do we see here? A perfect picture of leverage. God is light and there is no darkness in Him.[9] So when there was nothing but darkness, He leveraged Himself. He used light to its maximum advantage.

Can you see why it is impossible for a Believer to declare that they don't everything that they need? *"You will also declare a thing, and it will be established for you; So light will shine on your ways."* (Job 22:28 NKJV)

For when you don't have anything else to pull from, you always have the creative light and life of God inside of you. You are His walking duplicate; a lever of light. By speaking creative words, you can send the darkness of little into the light of abundance. So when things look completely empty, open your mouth and speak to the darkness, "Let there be light!" And watch while the revelation of the Word becomes a lamp and a light, shining on the path before you. The path that leads to more than you can ask or think.

What I've become convinced of is that most people don't understand *how* to appropriate leverage to their advantage. Or they see it as a big word that only financial gurus use to describe how really smart people make money. In actuality, leverage is so simple that even newborn babies come out the womb operating the tool of leverage.

How's that you may ask?

Once a baby realizes that when he or she cries, someone will

---

[9] 1 John 1:5

come to pick him or her up and cuddle them, guess what? That baby will use this newfound leverage, and cry in order to be picked up every time they want your attention. And if you think about it, crying becomes the only thing a baby can *use to its maximum advantage* until other forms of communication come to full development.

God expects us not only to have the right, but the responsibility, to leverage the tangible and intangible resources that God has placed in us from the beginning.

The problem is that many people don't recognize they have anything of value to use as leverage in the first place.

## Lessons Learned

*"And He looked up and saw the rich putting their gifts into the treasury, He saw also a certain poor widow putting in two mites.*

*So He said, "Truly I say to you that this poor widow has put in more than all; for all these out of their abundance have put in offerings for God, but she out of her poverty put in all the livelihood that she had."* (Luke 21:1-4 NKJV)

I must tell you that I didn't see the poor widow to be an example of leverage. As a matter of fact, when she was first dropped in my spirit, I didn't see anything that made this woman worth mentioning to you, beyond the usual discourse around these verses. Most of the time, this woman is tied to a sermon on faith and giving of offering. But leverage? I just didn't see it ... Until one day I did!

In truth, I had to look at this widow closely. I really didn't have any other choice. Jesus stops what He is doing and recognizes her contribution in the sea of participants that were giving great sums of money. We know that because they gave out of their wealth. So even a small percentage calculated to a substantial offering.

However, Jesus didn't focus on that. Instead He shined the spotlight on a few other attributes I believe will help us shape not only who we are, but also what we have in terms of life and leverage.

1. Quality over Quantity

Some of the best books I've ever read were considered 'small page count.' Why? Just because a book has a lot of pages, doesn't mean it gives a lot of information.

Jesus brought attention to the fact that the quality of her quantity was more significant than all those giving large quantities of low-quality gifts.

My wife loves chocolate. But I've always noticed that the higher the quality of the chocolate she eats, the less of it she wants. Why is that? Because the better-quality chocolate satisfies her desire more quickly. The quality is concentrated so that the indulgence satisfies her craving almost immediately.

The same is true for clothes. Well-made garments last longer and fit better. If a suit has been crafted with quality fabric by skilled hands, fewer alterations need to be made in order to achieve the best fit. Quality was crafted into every stitch of it from the beginning.

We see here that the quantity of her gift wasn't as important as the quality of the person who gave it.

   2.  Forget the Crowd

Don't get caught up in watching the crowd. I believe this woman was completely focused on giving her offering. I believe she had the 'eye of the tiger.' Her heart was fixed on her motivation to give, not on what others around her were doing.

Why? Because she didn't consider the size of her gift compared to that of others. It didn't matter to her who was standing in front of her in line or who was standing behind her. The only thing that mattered was that she had the opportunity to put those two mites in that basket, which is exactly what she did.

The crowd can serve as a distraction of massive proportions for those whose hearts are not fixed on doing the will of God. These people are easy to recognize because they never get anything complete. They let little things throw their attention off into left field when they should be tossing the ball into right.

> Genuine devotion is always better than generic praise!

Crowds are dangerous in that way. A crowd can move your attention from a productive mindset into a hypnotic state of the menial.

This poor widow didn't allow shiny jewelry and extravagant attire to detour her devotion and neither should we.

Always remember to keep at the center of your heart that a quality gift outlasts the hollow devotion of empty words and false actions every time.

3.  Let God Speak for You

There is not one indication in scripture that this woman even knew that Jesus had witnessed or commented on her gift.

Think about it.

Nothing. Nada. Zero.

If you read the same account in Mark 12, the verses explicitly tell you that Jesus was talking to the disciples.  He didn't even speak to her directly!

*"Now Jesus sat opposite the treasury and saw how the people put money into the treasury. And many who were rich put in much.*

*Then one poor widow came and threw in two mites, which make a quadrans. So He called His disciples to Himself and said to them, 'Assuredly, I say to you that this poor widow has put in more than all those who have given to the treasury; for they all put in out of their abundance, but she out of her poverty put in all that she had, her whole livelihood.'"* (Mark 12:41-44 NKJV)

Sometimes we forget that God is watching. But even more than that, He is speaking on our behalf!

The poor widow gave a gift so extravagant in heart that she got God's attention and He couldn't keep what He saw to Himself. Can you see the incredible gesture this woman's gift was in the grand scheme of things?

She wasn't the only poor widow out there. But there was something so special about her silent devotion and purity of purpose that it touched the heart of God. **Rest assured that when you touch His heart, He opens His mouth.**

That's where we all make mistakes sometimes. We want to touch money, houses, cars, and lands. While our aim should be to touch Him in everything we do.

She touched Him, and He tapped the disciples, the men who were being completely transformed by their intimate time with God on earth. He used a single, poverty-stricken woman to teach them how to give God all they had available to them. She was a living example of not withholding anything back. She was silent and let her offering give voice to the dictates of her heart.

---

I'm all for reciting confessions and speaking the Word over things in your life. But I believe that there is a time to give your vocal cords a rest and let the worship of your works trigger an auditory response from the mouth of God to the conditions in your life.

## Hard Lessons

What happens when what you have is not enough to produce anything? You give what you have to God. A poor widow threw in *"two mites, which make a quadrans*[10] *..."* Those two mites equaled less than a penny, but that didn't matter, because she placed them in the basket anyway.

The motive of a middle-class mindset is always focused on what will be received first. But this woman's act displayed a lack of concern for her own well-being. This is a volcanic departure from the core conversation of the message of faith today. Jesus didn't verbally document that she asked for anything. He only documents that she was willing to give everything.

This is our challenge today. One that demands each of us to ask the same of ourselves. Are we willing to give everything while the throngs of people around you are crowded in giving the least of their resources and even less of themselves?

I don't need to know your answer, but you certainly do.

I must answer for myself and you must answer for yourself. There is nothing gained by hiding the scales of our desires away from the light of God's judgement. He already knows. We can only do what the widow woman did and place the purity of what we have in His hands to replicate and redeposit in us as He sees fit. As I started to shift in my seat,

---

[10] John D. Davis, *A Dictionary of the Bible*

I realized that the potency of these verses was almost more than I could process at the time. And the more I watched this offering scene in my mind, the more questions seemed to emerge as I witnessed what happened that day in the theater of my heart.

## A Lineage to Live By

Then I wanted to know the obvious!

How did she have the faith to place those mites in the basket in the first place? And then it came to me out of nowhere.

*"By faith Sarah herself also received strength to conceive seed, and she bore a child when she was past the age, **because she judged Him faithful who had promised.**"* (Hebrews 11:11 NKJV)

She had a lineage to live by. One of her direct ancestors, named Sarah, herself had received strength to judge God faithful. The widow looked back to the testimony of a woman that came before her, where God spoke directly to what she had to work with. For at the time Sarah had the organs to conceive a child but they weren't able to produce anything of substance. Sarah had judged God faithful and look at what He was able to do. Instead of what her barren body was able to produce.

Those two mites were nothing compared to fruitless

fallopian tubes and old ovaries. If God was able to take what Sarah had and by His power gave her what she wanted most. I believe that poor widow could release the same faith that day and produce whatever she wanted or needed.

This woman became the poster child for possibility. She didn't have a penny to give. She had a mite. And for all intents and purposes a mite was the distant cousin in value of the American penny. She used the smallest thing to demonstrate a monumental faith, an enduring love, and a lesson on leverage that still teaches scores of pupils, even to this day.

*"And He looked up and saw the rich putting their gifts into the treasury, He saw also a certain poor widow putting in **two mites**."* (Luke 21:1-2 NKJV)

Can you imagine the courage it took for her to stand there with all those wealthy donors in their expensive garments and luxury garb?

Look at the picture. You had the area's most influential, wealthiest members of society putting their money in the treasury. Then here comes this poor widow.

She walked up there with no husband and no money. Now that's boldness!

This was a public venue. Everything and everyone was on display. There was no such thing as hiding your assets. God was standing there to witness your wealth and confirm your worship.

With that picture in mind, this poor widow sticks out like a sore thumb!

Where in the world did she come from anyway? Didn't they have another line for the poor to deposit their offering? I mean that way they would at least have felt better about the little they had to give, right?

Wrong.

There is no such thing as a secret worshipper. You can't hide your movements under a rock. Neither can the intentions of your heart be hidden from the One and True God.

Jesus wasn't standing there to condemn anyone. He was there to confirm the Word!

*"The Spirit of the Lord is upon Me, Because **He has anointed Me to preach the gospel to the poor** ... to set at liberty those who are oppressed; to proclaim the acceptable year of the Lord."* (Luke 4:18-19 NKJV)

Jesus was standing there to preach the gospel [good news] to this poor woman. He was there to confirm her wealth was not in how much she had, but how she used, or leveraged, what she had.

Remember leverage is using something to its maximum advantage. And Jesus was showing all those there that when this woman gave all she had for God, she was leveraging her assets like a pro. Placing her substance in the hands of God is giving it to the greatest financer ever.

*"... to set at liberty those who are oppressed ..."*

Remember what I said about poverty's persecution Oppression is the same thing essentially. Not having a husband was not what was oppressing her. It was her poverty that was stopping this woman from moving in the full flow of what life had to offer.

I believe that God didn't give a separate line for the poor to give because in the mind and heart of God, they all deserved to be in the same line. In God's mind there are only two classes of people—those who have been redeemed from the curse of the law, and those who haven't.

Maybe some of you are saying, "Look preacher, I don't have much more than two mites to give myself. How will I survive if I give all I have?"

My simple answer is, "You'll do just fine."

## Giving your Gifts to God

Someone I recently spoke to shared with me how much God has been requiring of her gifts lately. She essentially equated this period in her life as a dying or death. I have watched with great regard that this person is indeed experiencing a dying of herself. Because everyone will be given the invitation to die for Him.

I was. She is. You will.

I have no doubt that when the process of death is over that she will be more alive to Christ than she has ever been.

More aware of His presence in her than even she knows right now.

What she is doing in her actions is parallel to that of the poor widow in a sense. She is putting all she has in the basket. Yes, there are others with more to give, but what she has no matter how insignificant to others, is all she has to offer right now.

It's her livelihood. She isn't using it to get rich. She's not using it to have a spotlight shined on her. Instead, she is hidden away and polishing her gifts. In her mind, if this is all she has to give, then she wants it to be displayed in the best way possible.

She is leveraging her little in the hands of God.

## Handle with Care

In the Contemporary English version of Luke 21:1-2 it reads, *"Jesus looked up and saw some rich people **tossing their gifts** into the offering box. He also saw a **poor widow putting in** two pennies ..."*

The picture is clear. The rich people that were standing there didn't regard what they were giving with high value, because what they were giving wasn't going to make or break them. Hence, they ***tossed*** in their gifts as if they were of little value.

But what was no big deal to them was a monumental moment for her. So instead of tossing her mites, she placed them in with care. Carefully laying them in the offering basket.

She took her time and with great reverence she was laying herself in the box. Her acts were counting God faithful because who knows when she would have more to give again.

The poor widow was taking maximum advantage of what she had to leverage. Her little gift was being placed in the best possible scenario to produce results for her. She was ripe for worship and I would like to believe that how she offered her gift was more important than her giving anything at all.

## Use What You Have

*"For it will be like a man going on a journey, who called his servants and entrusted to them his property.*

*To one he gave five talents, to another two, to another one, to each according to his ability. Then he went away."* (Luke 25:14-15 ESV)

I read these verses and almost couldn't contain myself. I started thinking about the care that poor widow took in placing her mites as an offering to God. Then out of nowhere revelation came!

I had been asking how could she be so reverent with so little? Didn't she have some resentment because she was a poor woman with no husband. I was wondering what kind of a woman was okay with standing there in what probably amounted to rags, while others were dressed like royalty.

And then I went back and read this:

*"To one he gave five talents,* **to another two,** *to another one,* **to each according to his ability.** *Then he went away."* (Luke 25:14 ESV)

She was reverent with the TWO mites because she realized how blessed she was to have more than ONE to offer before God!

Her understanding was far beyond her years. Jesus had not taught the parable of the rich master yet.

I was stuck on the two mites more than I was the fact that God was not unjust! He had given to her according to her ability to leverage what she had.

Follow me. This was not about her being poor or being a widow. Jesus was not focused on either of those things in His reference of this woman. He focused on her capacity to maximize what she had!

It wasn't the amount; it was in her capacity to take what she had and place it in the best possible position to produce for her. Walking away from that offering box was a declaration of her understanding of leverage. She had just demonstrated the power of both tangible and intangible leverage and it came straight from the heart of God!

We teach, "Give God a percentage of what you have and keep some back for yourself." We are taught this because many believe that's how God is going to meet people's needs.

The principles of tithing and first fruits had been instituted in Israel for hundreds of years prior. Nothing new about that. Most of the churches today teach that. But this was an all or nothing proposition.

When was the last time you gave to God all or nothing? All your faith or nothing at all. When is that last time you stood before the altar of God and said to God, "I'm using all my gifts, talents, and abilities to further your agenda?" When?

I've watched people walk away from a good paying job or fabulous career to start a business. I mean they went in sink or swim. Completely dependent on the outcome of their balance sheet.

Many of them, by sheer will survive until they were able to reach the level of business success that they had hoped for. Because people will leverage whatever is at their disposal to get an outcome when they are truly committed to an idea, entity, or person.

The widow had been sold on God's ability to provide for her. How? Because, *"she out of her poverty put in all the livelihood that she had."* (Luke 21:4 NKJV)

Those mites came from her talent or ability in this case. She was going double or nothing with God.

*"So He said, 'Truly I say to you that this poor widow has put in more than all.'"* (Luke 21:3 NKJV)

When she walked away from that offering basket with nothing, she was essentially walking away with everything.

Her gratitude was the driving force behind her lesson on leverage.

There are some greedy, selfish, self-centered, spoiled people in this world. Living in an illusion that if they don't do it, then it won't get done. Get over yourself. Life is a gift and love a privilege. Stop with the nonsense.

Her life wasn't in the two mites it was in the God who had already multiplied the one she had in the first place.

She took leverage to the next level here by activating a principle that Jesus hadn't released yet. How do I know?

This woman places TWO mites in the offering basket at Luke chapter 12. Jesus doesn't share the parable of the talents until Luke 25!

*"And likewise he who had received **two gained two more** also."* (verse 17)

*"He also who had received two talents came and said, 'Lord, you delivered to me two talents; look, I have gained two more talents besides them.' His lord said to him, 'Well done, good and faithful servant; you have been faithful over a few things, I will make you ruler over many things. Enter into the joy of your lord.'"* (verses 22-23)

She got inside information that God will give a 100-fold return on whatever is given to Him, based solely on the condition of a person's heart. Making this poor widow a prophetic pioneer demonstrating the power of provision when you are in covenant with God.

## Fast and Loose

Finally, there is one last thing that I need to cement in your heart. Just because Jesus indicated that she was financially poor when she placed the money in the offering, doesn't mean that she stayed that way.

Remember He came by His own admission to preach good news to the poor and to set free those who were oppressed. There's no way Jesus is going to bring attention to this woman and she stay in the same place socially, financially, relationally, or spiritually after that.

I don't believe it!

Just like He used the man at the pool of Bethesda to showcase the power of the "I AM" at work, I believe the same is true for this poor widow. Remember everything changed for the man at the pool because *Jesus saw him* sitting there. Therefore, what would make us think that the same wasn't true for this widow?

Afterall, she didn't make an excuse. She didn't use her poverty, grief, or marital status as a crutch. She wasn't sitting or waiting on anyone. Jesus indicated she had a livelihood. Yes, He indicated her financial limitations, because He wanted to make an example out of her.

That day, she had supernaturally pushed the bounds of giving beyond anything that had been displayed to that point. She prophetically placed a demand on God to take care of her beyond her ability, by giving everything she had back to Him. Her actions exposed the heart of every man and woman there that day—including the disciples who had walked intimately with Jesus every day.

I dare you to go all in for God today. Use your money, abilities, faith, and love, and go all in on spiritual things. Then come back and tell me if the woman stayed poor after she walked away that day.

God leveraged the life of His Son to get the maximum advantage for humanity.

I know business owners and Wall Street have convinced you that the concept of leveraging was something they invented out of the brilliance of their minds.

Not even close.

If you learn how to leverage what God gives you, it leads you to places where only the Spirit can take you. Not to mention, your economic viability stems directly from your skillful use of leveraging your expertise and skills. If you do, it creates a life that aptly reflects the will of God purposed for those who indenture themselves to Him.

Why rely on luck when you were born with the power to leverage your latitude and longitude in life? The power comes with a surrendered heart and a submitted life.

## Chapter Seven
### A Rich Slave

The awareness of class can be in some ways quite disturbing. We reinforce to our children at a very young age to separate objects and people by those that have and those that do not. They understand the differences between rich and poor before they can even tie their shoe laces most of the time.

I'm sure that some would disagree with me, but I believe it's the right thing to do. I believe in making the distinction, because you have an opportunity to teach children God's concept of stewardship early on. In addition, if you are a wise walker of the Word, you also see these as times to share, encourage, and reinforce God's message not only to the poor, but *for* the poor.

After all, it was the disciples that Jesus was addressing when He said, *"For you have the poor with you always ..."* (Matthew 26:11)

There will always be those who are:

- Poor in heart.
- Poor in spirit.
- Poor in finances.

This speaks to the importance of equipping our children with God's instructions on ministering to the poor. It's a great concern to God and a serious responsibility for you as a parent.

## Desert Discernment

There are some very important reasons to teach your children the difference between rich and poor; theoretically and spiritually. And here's why.

You see, there are times they could be talking to a rich person who actually looks poor. I'm going to take this slow and steady with you.

If a person had encountered Joseph while he was standing on the slave block, it would have been very hard to explain the concept that this man was rich. Why? Because we are conditioned to function with people by what we see with our eyes and not with our heart.

However, if the same person saw Joseph again standing in Pharaoh's court then they would say, "Now this man is rich!" This all depends on how you classify rich. He was rich in the pit. He was rich in prison, and he was rich in the palace.

The same dream was alive in him all the time. The wealth

that was part of that process wasn't fully manifested, but you can't call a man poor necessarily because a man is not wearing the evidence of his wealth on his back.

As a country music fan, I'm always intrigued by how wealthy many country music stars are. I mean they sell out concert venues, sell multi-platinum albums, and amass great sums of wealth. But when you see them on television or at fancy events, they have on denim jeans, cowboy boots, and a tie!

No custom, tailored suit or diamond crusted cufflinks. Just jeans, a shirt, a tie, a cowboy hat. And if you don't have a discerning spirit, you will think that someone is poor when they are truly rich. Because what you see can deceive you ... if you're not careful.

*"Then Joseph said to his brothers, 'I am Joseph; does my father still live?' But his brothers could not answer him, for they were dismayed in his presence."* (Genesis 45:3 NKJV)

Be careful what you invest in.

From the first dream to his last breath, Joseph's heart was to invest in people. Yes, he acted like an immature brat when he had the dream about his brothers bowing to him, but he didn't understand that the bowing was not about him at all. It was about God.

God was going to elevate him to a position that would require him to serve his family in a greater way, and He was going to use his elevated position of prominence to do so.

Most people look at the dream the way the brothers did. They saw themselves bowing down to Joseph. They didn't see Joseph bending down for them.

Which is why anytime I see a worthless leader, I see a person who doesn't understand servitude. If he or she understands administration, but doesn't understand people, they are not fit to lead. Because power without compassion makes men and women pious dictators instead of pliable pastors.

I've had civic and religious leaders come to me with the same question for nearly 50 years. "Why can't I get people to follow my lead and support my vision?"

My answer is always the same. "If you don't love people, you shouldn't lead people."

Even the followers of cult leaders feel 'loved' by the crazy crusader in question. People don't follow people they don't believe love them and have their best interests at heart with sincerity and passion.

> Sometimes slavery can be worn on your back!

In grade school, I remember the names of the teachers that truly cared for me.

People come to Jesus for all sorts of reasons. However, they stay with Jesus after they have experienced the love of the Father through the sacrifice of the Son.

Joseph was able to lead a nation, including its leader as a purchased slave, because everyone in Egypt watched Joseph display his love for his God by his service to their country.

And for every businessperson, leader, and parent, that's how you live as the head and not the tail in life. Invest in people, not in things. Because people will happily do things, bring things, and accomplish things for a leader they love.

## Chapter Eight
# The Power of Privilege

*"Maybe she's born with it ... maybe it's Maybelline."* ®

In the mid-80's you couldn't turn on a television without hearing this jingle. I'm not sure why the little catchy jingle dropped into my spirit. But I couldn't stop thinking about the power of the privileged.

Privilege wields power. Think about it. Children born in the households of the affluent, have greater access to education, travel, social status, health care, money, and power.

They can easily take actions and make movements in their own life and also over people who don't have the same access. What privilege affords them more than anything else is preferred treatment in given circumstances of life.

American Express® sold its finance products based on advertising campaigns with the slogan, *"Membership has its privileges,"* from 1987-1996. What were they saying? They were saying that holding an AMEX® gives you access to <u>preferential treatment</u>.

Consequently, those who held the card felt a sense of power and pride. Many of those who didn't have the card, aspired to be approved for membership to this perceived exclusivity one day.

You see, it's all about perception.

## Perceived Power

*"Then Pharaoh said to Joseph, 'Inasmuch as God has shown you all this, there is no one as discerning and wise as you. You shall be over my house, and all my people, shall be ruled according to your word; only in regard to the throne will I be greater than you.' And Pharaoh said to Joseph, 'See, I have set you over all of the land of Egypt.'"* (Genesis 41:39-41 NKJV)

When Joseph was in the palace, he was afforded the privileges of the affluent. Afterall he rose to a position of prominence so lofty, there was only one man in all Egypt that wasn't subject to him, Pharaoh. Even his old boss and previous slave owner, Potiphar, was subject to his words. Some would say, now that's power!

But guess what? You're forgetting something.

He was still a slave.

Egypt was bowing its knee to a man in figurative, if not literal stocks and chains. He was owned. He had been bought and paid for. And with all the influence that the palace provided, he couldn't purchase his freedom from his master since it (his freedom) was never put up for sale.

He was out of the pit, no longer in prison, entrusted with the most valuable kingdom in the world at the time—but the perks of his position didn't give him the power to purchase his redemption.

Which meant, his children were born slaves with gold shackles around their necks.

He was a man on top, living in the middle. Can you think of anything sadder than that?

I can't.

But what a powerful demonstration of the limitations of man before the redemptive power of the cross.

## Palace Perks

The systems of man will always fail. Because they operate within a fallen culture of sin. There is only one way for man to be free of the limits this world system has devised, and His name is Jesus.

We cannot get around Him. There is no reason to debate Him. And we cannot overshadow the potent power of who He is—whether you accept Him or not.

The truth is evident, and the fact remains clear that He is the One who sits on the throne of God. His way is not to tie you into a system that keeps you bound, while screaming that you are free. No. He is freedom personified.

The salacious lies that seek to keep you entangled as a submitted slave to lack and poverty, while you walk around in the riches of this world, is all smoke and mirrors. A parlor trick for the poor—a magic act where you watch the DOW, the S&P 500, and the NASDAQ while the cost of bread, food, water, and wind rises and falls by the demands of the damned.

*"Then Pharaoh said to Joseph, 'Inasmuch as God has shown you all this, there is no one as discerning and wise as you.'"* (Genesis 41:39 NKJV)

Pharaoh could not afford to set Joseph free. Because he understood what most Believers fail to grasp. That God will show you how to rule a nation, if you would submit yourself in honor to Him.

If Pharaoh had let Joseph go free, what would have stopped him from taking over the throne completely. Truthfully, Joseph was only subject to Pharaoh because he had 'papers on him.'

Pharaoh knew that if God had shown him how to save a nation and make him wealthier in the process, what was stopping him from taking what he already knew to take the kingdom for himself? Nothing!

Pay close attention to what I say now.

You have gifts, talents, and abilities that rival those of all around you. And you feel the leading of the Lord to step out and start your own enterprise. You sense the spirit of God leading you in that direction. You have a track record of performing and helping those around you acquire wealth in their chosen fields and businesses.

God is saying, "It is your time." Use the same wisdom, discernment, talent, and hard work you have used to help others grow to establish your own firm.

It was the word of the Lord that God gave Joseph to interpret Pharaoh's dream. And this is the Word of the Lord to some of you reading this book at this moment in time. Take this Word, allow it to confirm your faith to move forward, and walk in the anointing of God over your life from this moment on.

---

*"And Pharaoh said to Joseph, 'See, I have set you over all the land of Egypt.'"* (Genesis 41:41 NKJV)

Listen to me, the enemy will try and pacify you with power that he really doesn't have. What Pharaoh failed to realize in his 'revelation of God' was that he was merely a pawn to place Joseph in a specific position in the palace.

It was never his dream in the first place, which is why no one could decode it but God. Joseph didn't even have the key until God gave it to him.

*"To him be all power over all things, forever and ever. Amen."* (1 Peter 5:11 TLB)

Joseph was in the palace because that is where God wanted him to be. Everything else is semantics. There was no other reason for Joseph being sold into slavery.

But Jesus came so that we don't have to be forced into slavery, we get to fall in love with Him as 'love slaves' by faith. The confession of your faith in Him alone who is Worthy, indentures you into the Kingdom of God as a love slave to Christ, who gets to sit in Heavenly places with Him. Free to approach the throne of God without fear, doubt, or condemnation.

Joseph was purchased with coins and a purse. You were purchased with blood and a life. Understanding that you were paid for and made free. His sacrifice becomes so overwhelming in your heart until you willingly tie your life to His—with a spirit of gratitude and a flow of love.

The perks of our position come with the posture of our prayer life. Because who wants a palace if it doesn't have a priest.

## A Palace Without a Priest

*"Seeing then that we have a great High Priest who has passed through the heavens, Jesus the Son of God, let us hold fast our confession. For we do not have a High Priest who cannot sympathize with our weaknesses, but was in all points tempted as we are, yet without sin. Let us therefore come boldly to the throne of grace, that we may obtain mercy and find grace to help in time of need."* (Hebrews 4:14-16 NKJV)

As a believer in Jesus Christ, I implore you not to miss this message. Don't build anything. Don't undertake any endeavor, and don't look for anything, unless you go to your High Priest over the house of God!

Jesus is our High Priest, meaning He is over every other system of religious retribution. Don't buy the pagan lie that Jesus is dead and therefore, He has no authority, insight, or influence over the affairs of your life.

If you allow the systemic mindset of darkness to rule the decisions and actions of your life, you are destined to live without the benefits that come from His roles as both Priest and King. Ultimately, limiting yourself to the spiritual degradation of being ruled without compassion.

As the Body of Christ, we submit to His authority as King and partner with His power to rule in this earth. But if we forfeit the blanket of the blood of His mercy, there is no way we can be spared from judgement or represent His compassion with wisdom and righteousness in a world that is already beat to scorn by a plague of darkness, with no mercy to give.

Having access to the High Priest of heaven is what makes the difference in your daily interactions in your home, business, workplace, and ministry. To remove His intercession on your behalf, reduces not only your effectiveness, but also the elevation of your existence beyond the atmospheric pressures of earth to the boundless heights of heaven.

Wealth warrants the understanding of this truth, especially for those who are called by the name of the Only True and Living God. Nothing matters more than having a balanced perspective of both love and honor. Righteousness and truth. Judgement and mercy.

---

I say, build a business, a ministry, or a home as massive as the sky that reaches the peaks of Heaven. But if what you build doesn't have a High Priest that has passed through it, it is destined to fail.

As I thought about Joseph, at first glance one would think that there was something very strange by Joseph never becoming Pharaoh, especially with his popularity and obvious talents of persuasion and perseverance. Heck, if he was in the United States of America, we might even consider him for a presidential run.

But we wouldn't, and neither could Egypt.

He wasn't born there. He was a citizen, but he wasn't Egyptian.

Yes, Pharaoh had acknowledged that Joseph had a God. But that wasn't really that unusual since Egypt had many people worshipping many Gods. In Pharaoh's mind, Joseph's God *just happened* to be the one to get the job done at the time. He didn't promote Joseph because of some spiritual awakening. No, he promoted Joseph because he got results!

## Chapter Nine
## **Making Money Moves**

Recently, I heard someone say, "Money doesn't leave the earth. It simply moves from one person to another."

Wow! What a statement.

*"Thus says the Lord, your Redeemer, the Holy One of Israel: 'I am the Lord your God, who teaches you to profit, who leads you by the way you should go.'"* (Isaiah 48:17 NKJV)

Fact: The earth is the Lord's and the fullness thereof and they that dwell therein.[11]

Let's cut to the chase. No playing around with this statement. It's time to deliver your mental money barriers once and for all.

If you can reconcile the thought that money has fluid movement, without allegiance to anyone or anything, then money has no power! It can be moved around, shifted, and

---

[11] Psalm 24:1

leveraged for good or evil. And it will obey anyone that has the knowledge and understanding of its ability.

If money had power would it do the work of human traffickers and build wells for villages in remote parts of the world at the same time? Can a spring produce both fresh and saltwater at the same time?[12]

No. Money would choose a side if it could. But that's the point—it can't.

Then what's the secret of the money movement that I'm speaking of in this chapter. It's simple. Money only moves for those who know how to move it. And that only happens to the extent you are willing to increase your knowledge of how not only the systems of the world work, but how the system of God's Word works!

What does means what? **Knowledge** is the inside track to financial wealth on both sides of the aisle.

I hear people say, "I need to make more money." Theoretically, that is not a true statement. Instead they should be saying, "I need to move more money in my direction."

God echoes this sentiment in the Book of Proverbs, *"The wealth of the wicked is laid up for the just."* (Proverbs 13:22)

It's quoted all the time and then people run out to find a get rich quick scheme or take another job to *'make'* more money, missing the entire context of this verse completely.

---

[12] James 3:11

There's one thing I don't think many people understand. The world's wealth is held among a concentrated few.

I know you've heard the top 1% hold most of the world's wealth. But there are some who believe it's more accurate to say that the top 1% of that 1% hold most of the world's wealth.

## The Global Elite

It is said that this small number of extremely wealthy people, descendants of wealthy families in Europe and the U.S., own a major part of the material wealth of the world.

Having the concentration of wealth in London, which is the center of the world banking system, the central control that the original families exercise is passed down from generation to generation tracing back as far as the late 1880's.

Although labeled a 'secret club,' the Global Elite is a highly organized group that operates through a web of 'private' organizations. And with virtual control over the world economy, they determine the course of history by most standards today.

Some say that the Global Elite is a myth and doesn't exist at all. There are others who spend their lives focused on chasing the power cord that is this group to prove once and

for all that the New World Order is part of the grand design this group of individuals has strategized even to this moment.

I realize the thought of this group of elitists may strike fear in your heart. Even giving you pause in terms of living a life on top of the mountain, instead of at the bottom. Deciding instead to take an approach that says, "Who cares? It doesn't matter since only a small group of people own everything anyway."

But that's not God's way and you know it.

Remember, wealth? Wicked? Just?

*"A good man leaves an inheritance to his children's children, but the wealth of the sinner is stored up for the righteous."* (Proverbs 13:22 NKJV)

Some of you have been beating your head against a wall trying to figure out why you don't have one thing or another happening for you. Why you can't seem to get your hands on this or that.

Well, let's look at these problems through the lens of God's eyes.

There are three attributes of wealth that you need to understand.

First, wealth resides with those who don't tell everyone everything. The wise have discretion. *"Counsel in the heart of man is like deep water, but a man of understanding will draw it out."* (Proverbs 20:5 NKJV)

122

Second, it is through diligent, disciplined work that success is earned. *"He who has a slack hand becomes poor, But the hand of the diligent makes rich,"* (Proverbs 10:4 NKJV). If you can organize your work and stay diligent at it, you become rich.

Third, God will strategically place people in your lives to fulfill your destiny if you are tuned into the voice of the Holy Spirit.

Take hold of the promises of God, exercising His will and way of doing things in the world. By the way, don't use the control of the global elite as a cop out.

Wealthy people remain wealthy by exercising the principles in God's Word yet deny the power of God demonstrated throughout its pages.

Unfortunately, people have become master extractors of the truth they want from the Word of God and leaving the life that is in God's Word as a wasteful by-product preferring their own agendas and purposes to the will of God in their lives.

Wisdom, righteousness, sanctification, and redemption are all part of the life that Jesus died to obtain for you. But! And I say, "but" emphatically. The Bible tells us that the children of men are wiser, (and I would add wealthier), than the children of light. [13]

---

[13] Luke 16:8

Let's look at these three attributes of the wealthy that God has outlined in His Word to us, with a heart to employ these principles in our lives starting today.

1. Use your tongue with wisdom. (John 7:17; James 3:6-10)

Some things are to be shared with a select group of people at a specific time, and under certain circumstances. There are also things that God tells you for you to hold close to the vest. They aren't to be divulged. They are secrets that He only wants to share with you.

However, be warned. If you are a person that God speaks to about everyone else, but He has very little or nothing to say about YOU to YOU, I promise you that you aren't hearing all you think you are.

God's goal is to transform YOU into His image and likeness. He wants YOU to take on the mind of Christ that He placed within you when you accepted Jesus' sacrifice for your sins. Ultimately, He is coming back for YOU without spot or wrinkle.

Focus on taking action more than talking. People of wealth are typically people of discretion—yes, that's including the 'reality' stars you watch on television. Do you really think what you're watching is real? I sure hope not.

Those who have kept their riches are those who have learned the art of controlling what they know, how much they know, and when and to whom they make information available.

Yet, most of the time, believers don't take that same approach to things in their lives, including the moves they make with their money.

Learning to be prudent with your tongue is so crucial that in some professions where confidentiality is of such importance, that if broken it can lead a practitioner to censorship, disbarment, and even prison, under the right set of circumstances.

> *"You are snared by the words of your mouth."*
> (Proverbs 6:2 NKJV)

Don't imprison yourselves by your speech. *"Death and life are in the power of the tongue, and those who love it will eat its fruit."* (Proverbs 18:21 NKJV)

2. An Organized Life (1 Corinthians 14:40 NKJV)
*"Let all things be done decently and in order."*

I know of a person who couldn't take a job he really wanted and had prayed diligently for because he was unorganized. He didn't get all the required documentation in by the deadline, so he could be considered for the position.

What he didn't know was that someone had already decided he was the candidate they would give the job to by his resume and recommendations.

But it was the lack of order and organized behaviors with his time management, etc. that caused a real adverse effect in this person's life and ultimately his finances.

Living last-minute is a habit successful people don't have. People who don't plan their days achieve less overall. Those who have no systems in place rarely complete goals effectively and typically live as if they have a shot gun at their chest in order to get anything accomplished.

Let's go back to the beginning.

From Genesis 1:1—Genesis 2:4 we see that God organized His time.

Last minute-living is not characteristic of the wealthy. Planning has purpose and God demonstrates for us that He is a master at managing His time.

He organized His productivity by days or specific allotments of time. Then He separated those placeholders for us to observe and live by as well. There is much knowledge out there about how calendars evolved, but we can see throughout scripture that God used the sun and moon and as separator of time and space.

We have time to accomplish plenty of things, but one of the most powerful attributes of the wealthy is organization of the time allotted.

Time management and organizational qualities are so important that people make careers out of helping to manage other people's time.

Functioning with the mindset of who you are as a son and daughter of God, living and walking in the position you were created to occupy is going to require a shift in the way that you handle your time.

*"... Let God transform you into a new person by changing the way you think ..."* (Romans 12:2 NLT)

For some this is going to take a little longer than others. It all depends on the habits of disorganization that have taken hold in your life.

However, that shouldn't stop you from moving forward towards a system of organization that helps you manage your life in a more streamlined and productive fashion.

From budgets to babies, everything in your life can benefit from better organization, where dedicated places and purpose evolve.

3. Creating Strategic Partnerships (Proverbs 13:20)

God is strategic in the most potent sense of the word. He does so openly, not hiding His intentions.

*"'For I know the thoughts that I think towards you', saith the Lord, 'thoughts of peace, and not of evil to give you an expected end.'"* (Jeremiah 29:11 KJV)

I can't tell you how many times I have heard people quote and focus on this verse. And with good reason. It's certainly reassuring to know that God is thinking of peace and not of evil towards you continually.

I understand how you feel, because I too take comfort in that fact as well. But that is not the totality of His strategic plan and it is certainly not the only thing that He is thinking when it comes to you. Let's read a little further to extract the fullness of His heart.

The Amplified Bible says it this way.

*"'For I know the thoughts and plans that I have for you, says the Lord, thoughts and plans for welfare and peace and not for evil, to give you hope in your final outcome.*

*Then you will call upon Me, and you will come and pray to Me, and I will hear and heed you.*

*Then you will seek Me, inquire for, and require Me [as a vital necessity] and find Me when you search for Me with all your heart.'"* (Jeremiah 29:11-13 AMP)

Before your beginning, God has been putting together strategic relationships for you. His purpose for these relationships is to get you to a place that you will be enamored with Him and find Him to be your vital necessity.

Yes, His thoughts toward you are of peace. But that is not the real issue is it? What separates the categories of life for God are those who come after Him and those who don't.

He strategically initiated relationships with every Bible character that you see throughout the Old and New Testament. From Abraham to Moses. Joshua to David. David to Daniel and Jesus to Paul. Everything for the Father hinges on His strategic partnerships in the earth.

He demonstrated through the Son what it means to have a goal (a desired outcome) and then put partnerships in place to fulfill a common goal.

Did you think the disciples were Jesus' idea? No. That was the mind of the Father. He demonstrated how to create strategic partnerships in the beginning, by creating man in the first place. He wanted to fill the earth with more of Himself, so He created a couple of partners to do what?

They partnered with God to accomplish the goal of fulfilling the earth with more of Himself.

No self-help get rich this week scheme or 10 Days to More Money books is really giving you anything new. If you read the Bible and rely on the Spirit of God to teach you the scriptures, everything will be revealed to you. Including the secret things those self-help books can't teach you or show you through reading without revelation.

This is intended to help and encourage those who are righteous, good-hearted people who truly love God but are having a hard time moving into the next phase of what God has revealed to you.

My purpose here is to suggest to you a path to partnership. Make sure that your goal is that of God. What is it He wants to accomplish in your life? Then I would believe Him and seek the leading of the Spirit of God to strategically connect you with those who are like-minded in whatever area you are looking to excel in.

WARNING ALERT!!! Do not limit yourself.

God partnered with Pharaoh to deliver Israel and Pilot to sacrifice Jesus!

Why is it important for me to bring this to your attention? Because mature people understand that you don't have to like or agree with every person that God is going to use to get things accomplished in your life.

Some people are put in place to fulfill a very tiny role in a large production. However, if you are a person that is moved by your emotions, instead of being mandated by the mission, there is a chance you won't seize the opportunity that God has placed before your hands to fulfill His purpose.

**Learn to Discern**

Discerning or distinguishing the purpose of a person, place, or thing comes from spending time with the Spirit of God. I am 100% convinced of this fact. The more you spend time with Him in fellowship, the easier it is going to be for you to distinguish the intent of the people, places, and things that come into your life.

Remember wealth is not leaving the earth. But I do believe that it is bottle-necked in a smaller sector of society than we might believe. Regardless, that's not the end of the matter.

*"The earth is the Lord's and the fullness thereof; the world, and they that dwell therein."* (Psalm 24:1 KJV)

There is not one resource in the earth that God did not place here. Which means that wherever the wealth in this planet is located, regardless if it is being hidden by men, it can never be hidden from God.

Most faithful men spend their lives searching for the hidden treasures, resources and wealth stored away by the hands of other men. When instead, <u>their days would have been better spent, searching for the heart and hand of God</u>, who can turn the flow of wealth in the direction of those determined to do His will.

## Chapter Ten
## **Wielding Wealth**

Whathat I learned many, many years ago is I don't have to cozy up to the wealthy in order to have money come my way. Neither do I have to turn around thirty times until I become dizzy to attract wealth to me. None of that is necessary.

**God has a way of getting wealth to me and it all starts with these precious words.**

*"Thus, says the Lord, your Redeemer, the Holy One of Israel ..."* (Isaiah 48:17 NKJV)

If you have accepted Jesus as Lord, then He is your Redeemer. He is the financer of your faith. He bought and paid for you. He understands investments, purchasing, assets, and wealth management better than any stockbroker, investment strategist, or wealth guru on this planet.

How can I say that with such confidence? Because He has been managing His resources since before the beginning of time. As a believer, I am part of His investment strategy. He went all in on me at my lowest state before I was even conceived.

Talk about understanding the buy-low, sell-high investment practice.

When I receive Him as Lord and He functions in the role of Redeemer, ultimately buying back what already belonged to Him, it opens me up to hear what He says. My ears are no longer clogged with sin and saturated with iniquity.

> God never wanted us to dig for wealth. He wanted us to discover it!

What does that have to do with wielding wealth?

The moment I become part of Him, my position in the earth changes. I become an heir (or owner) of everything the Lord, my Redeemer, has access to and ownership of.

Everything belongs to Him, including money. Which means He can move it around as it pleases Him. The moment you take a new position in the Kingdom of God, you too can wield that same level of wealth management.

But.

Yes, there's a but here.

We need to have a talk about wealth management from God's perspective. Don't worry, it's not going to hurt too much, but I can't guarantee that it won't sting a little.

## Wealth Managers

I cannot tell you how many times I have sat through services and listened to preachers excite the crowd just by saying, *"The wealth of the wicked is laid up for the just!"*

Look, I have said it and preached this verse a thousand times myself. But, this book is about meat and manifestation. <u>I want to change your mind and propel your momentum.</u>

Have you ever wondered why the wicked have the wealth in the first place? Let's go to the Word.

*"So the master commended the unjust steward because he had dealt shrewdly. For the sons of this world are more shrewd in their generation than the sons of light."* (Luke 16:8)

Let's read the same verse in the Amplified version:

*"And [his] master praised the dishonest (unjust) manager for acting shrewdly and prudently; for the sons of this age are shrewder and more prudent and wiser in [relation to] their own generation [to their own age and [kind] than are the sons of light."*

I like to say it this way.

*"The unjust are wise when it comes to handling their business."* Period.

When you read this story, you see the man was:

1. Shrewd: artful, astute, of nice discernment
2. Prudent: wise; intelligent, frugal, economical

3. Wise: Discrete and judicious in the use or applications of knowledge; choosing laudable ends, and the best means to accomplish them

While most people read this scripture and focus on the fact that there was a rich man commending a dishonest and unjust person, I believe they miss the truth in this scripture all together.

The verse doesn't say the master was praising the man because he was unjust or dishonest. It says his praise came because of how the man handled himself with the resources of the master, *despite* being dishonest and unjust.

How many of you can say you have been shrewd, prudent, and wise with what God has given you charge over? Exactly.

God is about getting a return on His investment. Forget what you've heard, He wants His resources to be used wisely. In an orderly, and organized fashion, with clear objectives, and wise planning.

My ears start itching when I hear someone who has no skills, no goals, no wisdom, no talent, no discernment, etc., quoting that the wealth of the wicked is laid up for them. Guess what? For them, it is probably going to continue to be laid up too!

You are entitled to the wealth that the wicked has laid up, but you haven't positioned yourself to be a competent wealth manager. With that in mind, it wouldn't make much sense for God to move money in your direction would it?

I don't think so.

In the end, if you aren't wiser, more prudent, and shrewder than the wicked, then you would wield the wealth back to the sinner anyway. Not because that's what God wants at all. But it is what you allow, by refusing to become more astute with financial matters. Lacking discernment and taking economic measures whenever possible.

The Internet is full of information. Instead of watching sports, playing on Instagram, or focusing on Facebook, when is the last time you read an article, or took an online workshop, or registered for a class, to gain more knowledge in finance?

*"For rebellion is as the sin of witchcraft, and stubbornness is as iniquity and idolatry ..."* (1 Samuel 15:23 KJV)

If you know someone who has a better handle on their finances than you do, have you asked him/her a question about how to do just one thing regarding financial matters?

NOBODY knows everything!

Put down your pride and ask for help when you need it. It's not enough to go to the altar of God and pray. Yes, He will meet you there and speak to you through His Word. But ultimately, the end goal is that you hear and obey His voice.

Maybe He wants to direct you to another person who has the answers you need. No man is an island to himself. You must be willing to acquire knowledge and then apply the knowledge you receive. Ladies and gentlemen, this is what we call practicing wisdom, which is one of the things God is looking for before He starts moving money in your direction.

Your confession alone won't do it. Just like, faith without works is dead,[14] so is your financial viability if you don't prepare to receive, manage, maintain, and maximize the wealth of this world in the same manner the wicked do.

Yes, it's harsh to think God would not move money from wealthy people to the just. But guess what? Based on what I see, I don't blame Him.

I can tell you enough stories to last you a lifetime that demonstrate the instability of spiritual people with calloused hearts, who say they have confessed Jesus as their Lord.

On the other hand, I have also witnessed the unparalleled generosity of those who in truth have a heart to serve God with even the little they have. Yet, it never fails that when I watch and listen, I realize they are lacking not because their heart is not in the right place, but rather their actions. It's their actions that keep them in a cycle of poverty. If not corrected, their actions will keep them from the opportunity to be a wealth manager for the Kingdom of God.

### Back to the Beginning ...

*"Money doesn't leave the earth. It simply moves from one person to another."*

---

[14] James 2:26

The movement of money happens by the hand of God. It is His to do with what He wills. Yes, as a Believer, you do have a right to the wealth of the wicked. However, just because you have the right to something doesn't mean you have the readiness for it.

I like to use this analogy:

My grandson, Andrew II, is currently a toddler. Yes, he is one of the heirs to all that my beautiful wife, Viveca, and I have. However, I will not be giving him the keys to my car. Truthfully, someone would probably think something was wrong with me if I handed him my keys and expected him to drive.

Doesn't make sense does it?

Even though you are an heir of God, if you don't do the necessary things to grow in maturity and knowledge, along with learning how to appropriately apply the knowledge you've received, someone could question the sanity of God to entrust you with wealth that you are not ready to handle.

I know that might sting, but there is some good news here. You can make changes today to begin to demonstrate your desire to be a steward of the wealth your wicked counterparts are harboring for you.

Managers must prove themselves. As we discussed before: Why do you need a car from a company that you don't represent the interests of? I encourage you to pray and ask the Spirit of God to shine the light of His Word in your heart, giving you clear directives as to where He wants you to start preparing for your wealth management position in the Kingdom of God.

I believe that as you make steps to this end, you will begin to see money moving in a fluid motion into your life. When it does, as I know it will, be sure to write me and let me know the wonderful miracles that manifest in your life. Include how you are managing what you have in your hand with greater prudence, making smarter choices and applying more wisdom in your everyday financial affairs.

## Chapter Eleven
## A Hands-On Approach

The Spirit of God is always looking to restore truth to covenant people who have lost direction in any area of their lives. Your path will be recovered by the truth of God's Word—every crooked way will be made straight—spiritually, mentally, emotionally, and financially.

God wants us modeling the Word in every area of life; not only spiritually, but financially as well.

*"Be diligent to present yourself approved to God, a worker who does not need to be ashamed, rightly dividing the word of truth."* (2 Timothy 2:15 NKJV)

*"Thus says the Lord, your Redeemer, The Holy One of Israel: 'I am the Lord your God, Who teaches you to profit, Who leads you by the way you should go.'"* (Isaiah 48:17 NKJV)

Some of you are not profiting in life because you refuse to humble yourself and allow someone to teach you.

*"Knowing this first, that no prophecy of Scripture is of any private interpretation, for prophecy never came by the will of man, but holy men of God spoke as they were moved by the Holy Spirit."* (2 Peter 1:20-21 NKJV)

*"For precept must be upon precept, precept upon precept, line upon line, line upon line, here a little, there a little."* (Isaiah 28:10 NKJV)

The Holy Spirit has one primary ministry and that is to confirm Truth. The Word of God is not private or hidden from you. What you don't understand or can't figure out how to apply in your life, He is there to walk you through it step-by-step.

Many of you won't even attempt to get your life in order because all you can see is the mess present right now. The problem is not how things look at this moment. The real issue is that you are looking in the wrong direction. Don't be distracted by what is. Instead look to **Who** is.

No matter the condition, the Spirit of God can untangle your life and put you right where you need to be. Doing the things that please the Father and glorify the Son.

When Jesus stands and proclaims the Word about Himself, He explicitly declares that His first ministry is to the poor.

Remember the poor widow with the two mites? I've got news for you. She wasn't the only poor widow in scripture that God chose to make an example of.

Ruth was picking up leftover scraps from the harvest of another man's field after losing her husband, home, and citizenship. But it was her heart of faithfulness and submission to the leading of God through her mother-in-law, Naomi, that changed her life forever.

She was poor one day, then married to the richest man in her area the next. It wasn't about her knowing everything. The altered state of her life was tied to her ability to be teachable. She had to learn the customs, the language and new processes of handling and receiving provision for her and her house.

Single mothers, God sees more in you than you see in yourself. Don't allow discouragement to overwhelm you to the point that you give up on God. **Rely on His ability to teach you what you don't know.** And seek out resources available in the earth to help make your way straight.

Lack doesn't have to be your lot in life just because you are the sole provider for your home. If you humble yourself to the true Provider that is found in our Lord, I am confident you will see gains and multiplied waves of increase in your efforts that come straight from God's heart to your hands.

*"The Lord will **command the blessing on** you in your storehouses and in **all to which you set your hand**, and He will bless you in the land which the Lord your God is giving you."* (Deuteronomy 28:8 NKJV)

*"The Lord will open to you **His good treasure**, the heaven, to give the rain to your land in its season, and to **bless all the work of your hand** ..."* (Deuteronomy 28:12 NKJV)

Like I said, early in this book, I love to be around those who have their hand to something. And, I detest laziness with a passion. It is such a waste of God's greatness to see people not doing anything with what He placed in them.

## The Call to Create

As I thought about what I wanted to leave in the pages of this book, it was important to me to shine a light on some of the practical aspects of creating wealth. I wanted this book to shift mindsets from the aspiration of middle class, to one that has no limits of how far and wide-reaching God's plans are.

I don't believe that Jesus taking an occupation before starting His earthly ministry was an accident. Again, God is a chief strategist, and everything connects to the overall outcome of His desire to bring man back to His original purpose at the beginning of creation.

Jesus was set to restore man back to his relationship with God at the moment of *"... be fruitful, multiply, replenish, subdue, and have dominion."*[15] Right after man has an established purpose of what to do with his hands, satan comes to shift man's attention to acquiring, instead of building.

---

[15] Genesis 1:28

The principle importance of this is that I want to jar your mind. Understanding that if Adam and Eve wanted to build a sun porch to enjoy the sunrises and sunsets together, God had no problem with that!

Listen to me, they were the exact duplicate of God. They could have created whatever they thought they needed or wanted. They had the finest materials and the creative genius of God inside them. Nothing that pertained to them enjoying the gifts God had placed in the earth was off limits to them.

> Lack doesn't have to be your lot in life!

They were not only free to build, but God had encouraged them to do so, *"... multiply, replenish the earth ..."*

Your view of God is too small! I want to shout this from the mountain tops.

Do you think that satan created the technology that runs our systems today? NO! He does not! He can't create ANYTHING!!!! He is a dead spirit, limited to contaminating anything and everything in which he comes in contact.

Your mobile devices are not the creation of satan. You give him too much credit No, it was the creative genius of God housed in the spirit of a man that is multiplying. God's creative genius to entertain the world.

God has always honored ingenuity. He loves to see you building things and putting your mind to work. I believe He has the biggest smile on His face when you have a creative problem, or you want to build something, but instead of relying on your own capabilities, you come to Him asking for His direction and assistance.

I can't tell you how many times, while building this ministry or initiating a music project that I would come to a creative impasse. Not knowing what to do next. I would run to the Holy Spirit to get direction from the Father! He would not only give me the creative idea or concept for which I had asked, but He has always gone further in creativity and concepts than I even thought possible.

**Creativity is part of what it will take for you to rise through the mental barrier of the middle class.** In truth, everything you see was created from the creativity of God as it pertains to this life.

Are these comforts and conveniences being used for purposes that are outside of what God intended? Of course they are. But that doesn't remove the fact that God gave man an unlimited supply of creativity. It's up to us to use it to create an unlimited supply of God's provision for establishing His kingdom on the earth.

### Don't Look at the Picture with Natural Eyes

*"¹ There was a **famine in the land, besides the first famine that was in the days of Abraham**. And Isaac went to Abimelech king of the Philistines, in Gerar.*

*² Then the Lord appeared to him and said: 'Do not go down to Egypt; live in the land of which I shall tell you.*

*³ **Dwell in this land, and I will be with you and bless you; for to you and your descendants I give all these lands**, and I will perform the oath which I swore to Abraham your father.*

*⁴ And I will make your descendants multiply as the stars of heaven; I will give to your descendants all these lands; and in your seed all the nations of the earth shall be blessed;*

*⁵ Because Abraham obeyed My voice and kept My charge, My commandments, My statutes, and My laws.'*

*⁶ **So Isaac dwelt in Gerar.*** "(Genesis 26:1-6 NKJV)

I believe that the heart of God is to stress this point vehemently. <u>Don't look at the picture!</u>

I wish I could shake some of you right now. Looking at the image and circumstances around you will kill your dreams and snatch your vision like a robber in the middle of the night.

Looking at the circumstances around you will kill your faith one blink at a time. Trust me. I've seen it happen to many people over and over again.

This scriptural account starts off letting us know there was a famine in the land. Meaning, God knew that scarcity was the cycle of the day.

On today's news you might hear a few other catch phrases coined to drive you into a manic state of financial fear and uncertainty:

- recession
- economic downturn
- market decline

Listen, it's all part of the plan to get you to shrink back, stop believing, halt your progress, and turn your back on the promise of God to you.

Do you know one of the most effective ways the financial sector uses to push an economy to slow down?

Get on the news and say that we are in a recession. Can you hear the tires screeching?

As soon as someone jumps in front of a camera with a microphone in his hand and a title under his name, 'Financial This' or 'Economic Expert That' people become parakeets of propaganda. Repeating with relentless passion that we are in a recession, when nothing in their life indicates that God has stopped blessing them at all.

Suddenly, people stop spending and start hoarding and changing their consumption habits almost overnight!

But God is different! His thoughts are NOT our thoughts.[16] They are higher than ours. And in this verse, we see something absolutely mind blowing to the modern money mentality.

---

[16] Isaiah 55:8-9

God was saying to Isaac, *"Don't Look at the Picture! Don't you move a muscle."* (emphasis mine)

He acknowledged what was going on around Isaac, but He never told Isaac to attach his thinking to those in his environment.

His father had been through a famine before ... so what! God wasn't moved by what appeared to be lack in the land.

*"That which has been is what will be, that which is done is what will be done, and there is nothing new under the sun."* (Ecclesiastes 1:9 NKJV)

And He is not at all affected by what appears to be lack in your land. He is the greatest financer that you will ever know. HE OWNS EVERYTHING AND LOSES NOTHING!

He has financed the earth for thousands and thousands of years. Created systems for everyone to thrive and prosper. Then leaves on record how to continue to replenish what you need when you need it.

Nothing is outside of his financial reach. So, can you see how silly it is to go to God telling Him what you don't have? Or reciting how bad it is in your world? It's crazy, right?

Isaac was in what we would call a depression. A severe, long-term, steady decline or stand still of a financial system.

You would think that God would tell Isaac to get out of there since he needed food and shelter to live on. But it always amazes me that He tells Isaac to stay put.

He did the same thing with a woman with a little oil and flour (See 2 Kings 4:1-7). She is in the middle of famine and the prophet Elijah doesn't tell her to grab what she can and go to another place. He tells her to stay where she is and God uses him to provide for her even though her lack was so severe, she had resigned herself and her family to death.[17]

Now that's what you call depressed circumstances.

## The Blessing in Obedience

The key to what we witnessed in the verses above is that Isaac followed the legacy of his father Abraham. Abraham had dwelt in Gerar and now God was telling Isaac to do the same. If Isaac had been a man with a rebellious heart toward God and didn't follow His ways, I don't believe he would have survived the famine.

We can take great comfort in this occurrence. When we are living through a cycle of economic downturn orchestrated by the systematic whims and wishes of the wicked, know that God is in control of our destiny and will lead us through even the most dire or disturbing turn of events.

Isaac obeyed the Word of the Lord and stayed right there in Gerar under the favor and protection of a man that his father had cultivated the most unusual relationship with. There was history between the two. And that history of push and pull, misunderstanding and mischief, would be an umbrella of blessing that only God could have created,

---

[17] 1Kings 17:7-16

yielding a fruitful friendship perfect for a famine.

*"So Isaac dwelt in Gerar."*

Our obedience to God is ALWAYS where the blessing for our lives is manifested.

Listen to me ... ALWAYS!

Don't let anyone tell you different. The breakthrough for your business and the deliverance for your family is all tied to the same. It comes to you by imploring a corresponding set of actions, moving in obedience to the last thing God said to you.

Those five words set an explosive chain reaction into motion. I believe verse six was the seed he sowed to reap the harvest we read about in the verses below:

*"Then Isaac **sowed** in that land and **reaped in the same year a hundredfold;** and the Lord blessed him. The man began to prosper and continued prospering until he became very prosperous."* (Genesis 26:12-13 NKJV)

Okay, does anybody notice the standout element of this verse?

All this happened DURING AN ECONOMIC DOWNTURN!

Don't tell me that God won't give you something to sow when economic challenges come. Even if there is no dust on the ground to sow, He will give you an instruction to sow yourself in obedience and in faith. Just standing still as an act of your will is enough for God to accept as a seed to prepare you a harvest!

*"For God is the One who provides seed for the farmer and then bread to eat. In the same way, He will provide and increase your resources and then produce a great harvest of generosity in you."* (2 Corinthians 9:10 NLT)

The key for you and I today is to refuse to allow ourselves to get caught up in seeing without eyes. If you don't have God's eyes when the world is running around screaming restrictions and scarcity, it will become easy to get your bullhorn and start yelling the same rhetoric too. Even though you have confessed Jesus as the savior of your world.

A few years ago, the world experienced a recession, spurring severe losses, unemployment, and terror throughout the world. People in our congregation moved to other regions and states to find work just to survive. Many lost their homes. Families split and hearts took flight because of uncertainty and fear.

I understood the moves on the surface, but I also understand the faithfulness of our God. And for some I am sure that God would have had them stay right where they were. Albeit, circumstances were painting a picture of destruction, failure, and defeat right before their eyes.

I wish I could say that everyone stayed at what I felt was the leading of the Spirit of God. Unfortunately, I can't.

During that season, I often turned to these verses to counsel and console. Looking back is the best way I know to look forward in the face of God. He had been faithful to this nation, these people, His Church before. So there is no reason for us to believe He would not continue to do what He's always done.

Economic systems go through cycles of ups and downs. Just like the undefined patterns of life, we have highs and lows. But I've discovered the key is to remain steadfast.

Following the leading of the Spirit of God is what every believer in Jesus can hold themselves to. There is comfort and peace there. You don't have to indenture your life to a devilish agenda to destroy and maim everything that has been made available to you through your covenant relationship with Jesus Christ.

God's intention is forward motion. He is always about building with a boldness that begs for attention from those who refuse to believe the wonder of His power.

Isaac was working and reaping while people around him were living in lack and despair. Guess what? It didn't stop his actions not one bit. He kept on sowing and obeying, and in turn he provoked God to continue blessing and prospering what he put his hands toward.

And nothing has changed about that Kingdom system to this day!

Not one single thing.

## Begin to Build

Isaac responded as soon as the Word was spoken. He didn't sit back and think it over for three years before he moved towards building a future in the land that God said He was giving to his descendants.

If you think about it, why would he sow his gifts, talents, abilities, and occupational pursuits in another land unless God was planning to have him reap something from his work there?

*"Then the Lord appeared to him and said: 'Do not go down to Egypt; live in the land of which I shall tell you. Dwell in this land, and I will be with you and bless you; for to you and your descendants I give all these lands, and I will perform the oath which I swore to Abraham your father."* (Genesis 26:2-3 NKJV)

Living in a land and dwelling in a land means you plant yourself there. You become part of the fabric of that culture. You make ties there and you work there. God gives you clear instruction on your assignment there and you experience the blessing there.

The Lord was telling him where He was giving him permission to build. Did you hear me?

When you are in Jesus and He is in you, the Holy Spirit will lead you to the permissible area(s) or land(s) you can build in.

*"The Lord will send a blessing on your barns and on everything you put your hand to. The Lord your God will bless you in the land he is giving you."* (Deuteronomy 28:8 NIV)

Build where the blessing is. Some of you are stuck in a cycle of lack and defeat even when there is prosperity all around. Why? Because you aren't building anything.

The frozen fetter of mediocre thinking does nothing to create or curate a future the Lord can be proud of. Everything is tied to a relationship with Him. Yes, the modern mantra will tell you to go your own way. And I dare say, 'that's the problem!'

*"There is a way that seems right to a man, but its end is the way of death."* (Proverbs 14:12 NKJV)

God has declared the end from the beginning, and He has a blessing for you in a specific place. But ladies and gentlemen, you must put forth some effort.

That's right, I've said this many, many times before. Sowing takes effort and reaping requires work!

Yes, Isaac had the same promise of blessing the Lord had spoken to his father, Abraham. And yes, we are also able to ascertain that he was planted in a specific place or region to reap the blessing of that promise. But let me also tell you without hesitation, Isaac was still obligated to 'work' the promise.

God honors those who work to build things. Even Jesus, God in human flesh, took an occupation **before** He took a ministry. Jesus, a carpenter by trade, began His work by building with His hands.

I read somewhere that carpenters make anywhere from $21 to upwards of $55 per hour. Sadly, we don't teach our young people things like this. Instead, they fantasize about being professional athletes and social media socialites, instead of understanding that working with one's hands is honorable and places you in perfect alignment with the Word of God. (Deuteronomy 28:8 &12)

I believe since Jesus was sent to build the Kingdom of God on earth, He took a profession that reflected His calling. And I further believe if people select professions that lend themselves to their natural gifts, then increase is inevitable.

It's only the steel drum of the middle-class mindset that halts Heaven at making a living. This mindset never moves into mental patterns and bold behaviors that prompt a person to move beyond making a living to a heightened experience of making a difference with the abilities that God has placed inside them.

The movements of the middle class stop at the greedy hoarding of life for themselves. Never thinking of the horizontal mandate of maturation that comes from a heart in complete covenant with His will in the earth.

Isaac was the next tier of the blessing that God had promised to Abraham. He was the *"... and so shall thy seed be."* The promise personified.

What better person to show how the blessing of God and the call to create takes a hands-on approach, winning and working when the circumstances of environment and faith are challenged at their core?

Abraham started faith. Isaac continued it.

Famine is no match for faith. And builders reap the blessing of obedience by embracing a hands-on approach to the call to create regardless of the financial famine threatening to stand in their way. They plant themselves in the place of God's choosing. Where He satisfies the soul and matures the mind by exchanging their thoughts for His.

## Chapter Twelve
# Mind Over Matter

*"Let this mind be in you which is also in Christ Jesus."* (Philippians 2:5 KJV)

The only mind that matters is the one that has been renewed by the Word of God. When it comes to the middle class, nothing about it resonates with the heart of the Father, the mind of Christ, or the ministry of the Holy Spirit. Nothing.

Those who have settled into a norm of lack, a mindset that accepts the language of those living below the level God has designed, for His children, have chosen that lifestyle.

For a moment ... let's not look at what other people believe. Let's examine your beliefs. Where is your expectation? What do your words dictate in your life? For many your words have indicated your indifference toward the will of God.

### The Truth About Nothing

As I've said before, the Word of God is profitable. You can take the Bible, study it, and become the richest man or woman on the earth, if you apply the life that lives within the pages.

The middle-class mindset lingers around indifference to God's Truth. It is two-fold: What you don't know will hurt you. And what you do know, but don't apply will do the same to your life.

The entrance of God's Word gives light and understanding even to the simple or the one void of understanding. Which means the more you know, the more light you can access.

In contrast, the less you know, the less light or revelation you have. The less light, the more darkness (satan) can take advantage of in you. This truth is parallel in any area of your life.

The question you must ask yourself is not "What is light?" It should be, "Who is Light?"

Jesus is the light of the world.[18]

Nothing else on earth has the power to dispel darkness outside the light of Christ revealed to man in the scriptures. Therefore, until a man receives the revelation of this truth, he or she is destined to live beneath the privilege the Father provides to the Body through the Son.

**Give Me A Word**

God's Word is the only thing that produces the more abundant life. But in order to live in the executed reality of

---

[18] John 8:12

the fullness of God, your faith must be activated with an audacity that pricks the consciousness of those around you and shakes the forces of hell to its knees.

The audacity of faith requires boldness. A daring, unapologetic willingness to challenge assumptions or conventions, or tackle something difficult or dangerous. The sentiment is confidence, self-assurance, brashness, nerve, and imprudence.

The audacity of faith rejoices in the fact that God cannot or will not EVER break His Word.

Jeremiah 1:12, *"He watches over his word to fulfill it."*

Miracles don't just happen. They happen to people who believe. You're a miracle. But you don't want to say that because of what other people might think.

But who cares what other people think about you? Do you want to be a pulper all your life? Do you want to be sick or full of disease, living a hard, useless life all the days you are on this planet? Of course not.

You were meant to be a shining star. You are a manifestation of the Son of God. Hope is in you. Christ is in you! Life is in you.

*"Heaven and earth will pass away, but My words will by no means pass away."* (Matthew 24:35 NKJV)

*"Therefore, whoever hears these sayings of Mine, and does them, I will liken him to a wise man who built his house on the rock: and the rain descended, the floods came, and the winds blew*

*and beat on that house; and it did not fall, for it was founded on the rock."* (Matthew 7:24-25 NKJV)

Whether you are born-again or not, you're not sheltered from the storms of life. The storms will come and beat on your house. However, because you have built your foundation on the Word of God, you will not fall, and you cannot fail.

Moving beyond the middle happens the moment you realize Who lives inside of you.

Satan only deceives people who allow themselves to be deceived. And he will use anything at his disposal to halt you in your tracks. Resorting to shadows of inferiority, like race, gender, background, education or the lack thereof against you. Don't give any of that silliness the time of day.

Satan who is nothing more than a defeated spirit and an empty corpse is trying to distract you.

Latch on to God by faith. Turn corresponding actions into summersaults beyond that sort of nonsense. Stop acting like a middle of the road, lackluster manifestation of an insufficient God.

Every time you read the Word, you are reading about the One who defeated death and crippled hell. Triumphing over darkness and mastering everything in His wake.

And if you are part of His Body, you have accomplished the same feat and sit in the same position of authority. The issue is what will you believe today?

162

There is no right or wrong in this. The choice is yours. From finances to famine. The choice to live an abundant life is not something God is pushing on you. His desires toward you are clear. Crystal clear. But the middle should not be the stopping point of any Christian—it should be the springboard that launches you into the higher dimensions of God spiritually, socially, economically, physically, and financially.

The decision is yours.

## Chapter Thirteen
### In Sickness and Wealth

*"I **wish** above all things that though mayest prosper and be in health even as your soul prospers."* (3 John 2)

Sickness is as much about financial annihilation as it is physical impairment. When people read the above verse, it is usually thought of from a two-dimensional standpoint.

Dimension #1: God wants me to prosper.

Dimension #2: God wants my soul to prosper.

I left thinking, "Is that it?"

One of the most dynamic applications of this scripture is the word ***hope***. The apostle John was summing up his writings here. Ultimately, he was saying that he had laid out his case for Christ in the book of John, 1 John, 2 John, and now the conclusion of the matter is simply this:

*"I hope that you take everything that I've written and live a healthy life, physically.*

*I pray that you are not ruled by your emotions but stand strong in your faith.*

*Knowing that when you are strong in your conviction of the Christ, then everything else in your life is sure to increase exponentially."*

It's just that simple.

## Satan and Sickness

*"The thief comes to steal, kill, and destroy, but I have come ..."* (John 10:10)

Have you ever had the common cold? Sure you have. What is the first thing you want to do when you catch a cold?

Lay down and sleep. It's the first sign something is wrong with the human body. It ceases to be active. It refuses to move and expend energy. Even sitting up is a chore when you have something more advanced like the flu or pneumonia. And guess what? Laying down is exactly where satan wants you.

His goal is to make you defenseless and unable to care for yourself. He wants you weakened and wounded; worried and worn-out.

His aim is to kill you, but he doesn't want you to die with all your wealth intact. He places sickness in the midst of God's people to steal your life and drain your bank account so there is nothing left to leave your grandchildren.[19]

He wants to destroy the generations coming behind you. Not to mention, he wants the last memories your family has of you to be of you sick, diseased, in pain, etc. DON'T STAND FOR IT!

Jesus came so you would have LIFE!

Zoe. The life of God that can't be extinguished! Zoe life conquered death and transcends earth. You can leave this earth on your own terms, not on satan's.

I want you to hear me! You can leave this earth on your OWN terms—NOT his.

That is why you must be vigilant in the Word of God. Being focused on being a skillful warrior with the Word is the only way to stand against the wiles of the devil.[20]

## What's Your Issue?

*"And a certain woman, which **had an issue of blood twelve years**, and **had suffered many things of many physicians**, and had spent all that she had, and **was nothing bettered, but rather grew worse**, when she had heard of Jesus, came in the press behind, and touched his garment. For she said, If I may touch but his clothes, I shall be whole. And straightway the fountain of her blood was dried up; and she felt in her body that she was healed of that plague."* (Mark 5:25-29 KJV)

---

[19] Proverbs 13:22
[20] Ephesians 6:11

My God!

This woman was bleeding to death!

My heart was pricked when I thought about my wife, my daughters, my granddaughters and the women at my church. What if it was one of them in this woman's situation?

One of the things that stood out to me in this account is how she, *"... had suffered many things of many physicians, and had spent all that she had, and was nothing bettered, but rather grew worse ..."*

These physicians were draining this woman's finances and using her as a guinea pig in the process. She was nothing more than a lab rat to them. They didn't know how to help her, but it didn't stop them from taking her money.

I don't believe this woman was middle class by any stretch of the imagination. She couldn't have been. Her doctor's visits would have crippled most people's wealth after the first six months!

But she was able to go to the physician's office, have examinations, participate in tests, and endure procedures all without health insurance!

There was no co-pay or in-network or out-of-network care. She was underwriting her own healthcare while she was growing worse and bleeding more.

Satan wants you to endure sickness, so you keep spending your money to get help from physicians. They were stealing her money as fast as he was taking her life.

Now let me make this clear. I am not against physicians and I have the privilege of pastoring wonderful, skilled, gifted, and prayerful physicians and other medical professionals.

But my job is to make sure I declare to you that God has NOT placed sickness on you to teach you anything. He is not stripping your finances down to nothing and then saying, "Now have you learned your lesson?"

Lies.

Jesus died for not only healing if you get sick, but He died for health, so you don't get ill. He came to conquer everything that comes against your life of abundance and that includes more than money.

Sickness is oppression, pure and simple and Jesus came to release every captive. He came to set free those who are bruised, crushed by tragedy, and broken down by calamity.

This woman's health issue had broken her body and crushed her bank account; she refused to take a mindset of surrender to the societal expectations around her.

She had tenacity. Clinching to hope that in some way her body was going to be healed. Once she heard about Jesus, she pounced at the chance to get to her healing.

Mindset makes a difference when it comes to healing. What happens in the heart of person will ultimately determine whether they stay in faith or give up in surrender. I make that statement with as much compassion and tenderness as I can.

I have presided over funerals of some of the most faith-filled people in the earth, who simply surrendered their faith for healing on this side of earth in exchange for the blessed hope that we have in eternity.

## Wellness vs. Wholeness

*"... when she had heard of Jesus, came in the press behind, and touched his garment. For she said, If I may touch but his clothes, I shall be whole. And straightway the fountain of her blood was dried up; and she felt in her body that she was healed of that plague."* (Mark 5:27-29 KJV)

Of course, the account of this woman's healing was no doubt miraculous and lends itself to much teaching and many lessons.

I mean I could go on and on about how the health care system was designed to keep you sick. Our society has embraced illness to severely savage the saving and earning potential of the monetary middle class. It doesn't make money off the poor, and it's not utilized by the wealthy. It's the middle-class family that bears the burden of the ills of healthcare and the money mongers of medicine.

The wonder of wellness has swept the airwaves like a soothing balm. Everyone from health practitioners to hospitals are preaching the preverbal call to wellness. Leaving the condition of hopes shattered when a person near death realizes that they've been sold a bill of goods and that wellness doesn't compare to wholeness. Not by a long shot.

Making my point even more apparent is that this woman who we hail as a faith fireball had passed the point of wellness.

Surpassing the middle-class mentality that says, "Provide me relief from my crisis of the moment or meet my immediate need." By this woman's own confession, she wanted wholeness—a total restoration of everything she had lost.

## Total Restoration

There is a difference between being healed and being made whole. Healing provides relief and wholeness brings restoration.

I've heard people say she walked to Jesus upright and kneeled to get to His garment. I have even taught this from time to time. But let's be realistic for a moment. How much strength could the woman have had to stand, if she had been bleeding for 12 years?

I think it's more likely she was crawling to get to His garment because she knew if she made it that far, she would be made whole. I believe those words registered the logistics of her faith not the feebleness of her frame.

She had locked in on Jesus—pure and simple.

She had already given the doctors a chance and they had failed. Her loss was a multi-dimensional mash-up of medicine and money. But she pressed her way and relinquished her pride in order to reclaim her future.

*"... for she said, if I may touch but his clothes, I shall be whole."*

Ultimately, what Jesus did for her, He wants to do for you today. He wants to make you whole. He wants to stop the draining flow of your medicine cabinet for good. Refuse to surrender to the recession of your reality, by reaching into the reservoir of Heaven's restorative power to change your life on earth, beyond the confines of a class driven community of settlers. Moving into the abundant access of the Blessing that Jesus Christ richly provides to all those who believe on His Name.

Grab the truth that your body and your bank account are subject to a touch from the "I AM" when you reach out to Him by faith.

## Chapter Fourteen
### It's About Time

*"To everything there is a season, and a time to every purpose under the heaven."* (Ecclesiastes 3:1 KJV)

God gave us time for everything. There is nothing on this planet that God has not established a designated time for. Hence the reason why I believe time is man's greatest resource.

Not money. Time.

With time, you can make money. But money can't buy time in the literal sense of the word.

You might be wondering why I am allocating designated space in this book to discuss something as linear as dates on a calendar or ticks on a clock.

Because your life is wrapped in time. And until you elevate your mindset to respect the first resource that God gave man, you will never recognize the unlimited wealth that lies at the base of your fingertips every single day.

Most people allow time to go wholly unnurtured, and its wealth potential unrecognized until it has been squandered away. However, this does not have to happen to you. Dear ones, this is where the rubber really does meet the road.

I have said it over and over again throughout this book: "The middle class is about a mindset." And now is the time for you to break through those mental shackles for good!

Your emancipation from the middle class depends on your ability to receive the truth as it pertains to the manipulation and domination of your greatest resource—time.

## Don't Move

*"On the day the Lord gave the Amorites over to Israel, Joshua said to the Lord in the presence of Israel:*

***'Sun, stand still over Gibeon, and you, moon, over the Valley of Aijalon.'***

***So the sun stood still, and the moon stopped,*** *till the nation avenged itself on its enemies, as it is written in the Book of Jashar.*

***The sun stopped in the middle of the sky and delayed going down about a full day.*** *There has never been a day like it before or since, a day when the Lord listened to a human being. Surely the Lord was fighting for Israel!*

*Then Joshua returned with all Israel to the camp at Gilgal."* (Joshua 15:12-15 NIV)

You have been given dominion over time!

Thus, you have the ability to manipulate time to fulfill the purposes of God in your life. Time is something God made for the earth. Just like the fish of the sea and the fowls of the air. And I guarantee when you see a wealthy person, you see a person who has learned to manipulate time to his/her advantage.

And guess what?

So can you.

Joshua was not a born-again believer. Jesus had NOT died yet. Joshua demanded the sun and the moon obey him solely based on the promise God made over his life as Moses' successor.

I can almost start dancing about this. He believed the promise of God to him and demanded that everything, including the solar system, obey his voice because he understood he had an audience with God!

You shatter the leverage of the middle-class paralysis the moment you step into the understanding that you have an audience with God—the CREATOR of HEAVEN and EARTH!

God listened to Joshua through a veil that had not been torn yet.

You must get the revelation in this because it will change your life forever.

*"Then God said, 'Let there be light'; and there was light. And God saw the light, that it was good; and God divided the light from the darkness. God called the light Day, and the darkness*

*He called Night. So the evening and the morning were the first day."* (Genesis 1:3-5 NKJV)

The function of time was instituted on the earth by God. And he passed down the ability to dominate the established protocols of time on this planet from the beginning.

And even Adam, His most prized possession had complete dominance, living outside of the restrictions of time as long as he had an audience with God.

*"Then to Adam He said, 'Because you have heeded the voice of your wife and have eaten from the tree of which I commanded you, saying, 'You shall not eat of it. Cursed is the ground for your sake; in toil you shall eat of it **all the days of your life.**'"* (Genesis 3:17 NKJV)

## This is the Day

Adam didn't know the number of his days. And neither do you or I. God intended Adam to live forever, right here on this earth. God started a family, desiring a large brood to populate the planet with, people loving and serving His desire. As He walked through the cool of the eve enjoying fellowship with mankind lavishing them with good things.

No. Death was not part of the original life of man. He was never meant to die. And death had no place on earth until Adam surrendered his dominion over to satan.

Why do you think Jesus didn't just die on a cross and then ascend to Heaven immediately? Because He had some unfinished business. The keys of death, hell, and the grave had been surrendered into satan's hands and Jesus was not going back to Heaven without them.

## Access Granted

The Father wanted man to have the one thing Adam lost above all else that day in the garden. He wanted to restore man's free access to Himself. Because access to God gives you unfettered access to everything that belongs to Him; including time and substance.

*"Behold, children are a heritage from the Lord, the fruit of the womb is a reward."* (Psalm 127:3 NKJV)

God doesn't have limitations on what He has made available to His children. He is not only lavish in His love, but also in His goods for His offspring.

Why? Because love doesn't stop in the middle. There is no expiration date on the length or dimensions of time that my love for my children, grandchildren, and great-grandchildren will be displayed on this earth.

Even when the number of my days have expired here on earth, and I have transitioned to be with Him, my love will remain in every wind and breath. The moments will pause in our present form, but my love will endure in every whisper and every word.

And God the Father felt the same way, so He made a Way. The distance was too much for Him to bear, so He pulled out of Himself a way to be with us forever through a blood wrapped gift latched with love and tied with grace.

*"If you then, being evil, know how to give good gifts to your children, how much more will your Father who is in heaven give good things to those who ask Him!"* (Matthew 7:11 NKJV)

Of all the good gifts I have to give my children, time is not one of them. Only God has access to the commodity of time in the sense of days numbered for each man and woman on earth. But the 'good thing' is that He has restored to man the option of eternal life.

And what a gift it is.

As times increase in darkness on the earth, men and women will still have the option to choose where they will spend their time in eternity. Please remember that.

No matter what you see as the earth remains, you will always have the choice to choose God. You will have the option to accept the gift of Jesus Christ.

You can always choose to be a child of God filled with His Spirit. My prayer for every person reading this book is you don't let time run out without making a decision for Jesus.

*"And as it is appointed unto men once to die, but after this the judgment: So Christ was once offered to bear the sins of many; and unto them that look for him shall he appear the second time without sin unto salvation."* (Hebrews 9:27-28 KJV)

---

As a believer in Jesus, your wealth is tied to the access you have to the Father. Throughout the Old Testament, we see the key to every man's length of days and lavish life was tied to his or her access to God.

Adam lived 930 years even though he and his wife were kicked out of the garden for treason and sin.

Abraham lived to be 175 years old even though he lied about his marital status and essentially gave Sarah over to another man's bed. God was with him and he walked away with wealth, because he had access to the Father.

Even Sarah's body reproduced the wealth of a nation, because of her access to God; and strength entered her womb so that she could carry the lineage of a nation at 90 years old.

Isaac was 180 years old when he died, after being one of the wealthiest men on earth. Why? Because everything Abraham had was Isaac's. His father's wells and his instructions to him were the foundation of his inheritance.

Jacob only lived to be 147 because at his own testimony, his days had been evil before the Lord. Still he had a life of plenty because of the blessing of God over his life.

David's days were shorter, not because His love for God was less rich or relevant. I believe David was simply worn-out. Afterall, He had been fighting all his life. But at the end of his days, David had amassed a treasure chest of wealth so substantial that he single-handedly financed the temple construction as a monument of his devotion to his God.

And the list goes on and on.

I ask, will your name be among those who followed the pattern of devotion to God as the prelude to worship and wealth?

Today, we can't use the excuse that it's too hard. You can't hide behind your sex or your color. You can't claim you don't have access to what you need. Because as I have discussed with you earlier in this chapter, it's not about access to man, it's the access to God that makes the difference.

The fraternal order of heaven stems from the covenant relationship offered through the Son making all your flimsy excuses and accusations obsolete.

When Jesus invited the disciples to come follow Him, they were all businessmen with families, educations, and affiliations. Not to mention, He never told them how long they would be leaving their businesses behind. I mean these were successful men. But they changed their focus and took the opportunity Jesus [God] was extending to them for a one-on-one relationship that would ultimately change their lives forever.

## Leave It All Behind

*"Now behold, one came and said to Him, 'Good Teacher, what good thing shall I do that I may have eternal life?'*

*So He said to him, '"Why do you call Me good? No one is good but One, that is, God. But if you want to enter into life, keep the commandments.'*

*He said to Him, 'Which ones?'*

*Jesus said, '"You shall not murder," "You shall not commit adultery," "You shall not steal," "You shall not bear false witness,"* ¹⁹ *"Honor your father and your mother," and, "You shall love your neighbor as yourself."'*

*The young man said to Him, 'All these things I have kept from my youth. What do I still lack?'*

*Jesus said to him, '**If you want to be perfect**, <u>go, sell what you have and give to the poor, and you will have treasure in heaven; and come, follow Me.'</u>*

*But when the young man heard that saying, he went away sorrowful, for he had great possessions."* (Matthew 19:16-22 NKJV)

As I thought about breaking through the mindset of mediocrity I was as surprised as you are that the rich young ruler came to my heart.

At first glance I couldn't make the application that a rich young man would be an example of the hindrances that prohibit the middle-class mindset. After all, from the outside looking in, he seemed to have everything going for him:

1. He was rich.
2. He was young.
3. He was a ruler (leader).

But then I realized that in his case, the money, youth, and authority he had was obviously not enough. I mean he is the one who came to Jesus asking what he needed to do to acquire eternal life.

Wealthy people are always on the lookout for something to acquire with their wealth in order to get more wealth. More riches. More acquisition of things, people, position, and power.

I had never really looked at his question from that standpoint before. But somehow the response that Jesus gave makes more sense to me, now more than ever.

The invitation and instruction were two sides of the same coin. Jesus was saying, "Go master your mindset and then come back and follow me."

Yes, the man was rich, but his mind was poor. He could not grasp that selling what he had and giving to the poor was not about him having wealth. It was about wealth having him. And then it dawned on me.

The person who thinks poor doesn't believe he or she will ever regain what they have if they happen to lose it all. It's fear-based thinking.

The media will have you think the middle class of our society is doing everything they can to get out of the middle-class category, trying to grow themselves and build more wealth for their families. But I don't believe that's true.

This is what I came to attack with these pages. Some of you move too quickly, chasing what is the next scheme or opportunity or promise for wealth and riches. And in doing so, you walk away from the very person that has the ability to give you all your heart desires, if you would just follow Him.

I'm saddened when I think of those who remind me of the rich young ruler. Those who I see every day, who walk away from God to pursue or hold on to what they have instead of selling what they have acquired to follow after Him.

He was asking him to sow a seed into his own life. By selling what he had and giving to the poor, he was sowing seed into the very ones that Jesus came to preach the gospel to.[21] It would have been his first official act of ministry, if only he had been able to discern it.

*"And everyone who has left houses or brothers or sisters or father or mother or wife or children or fields for My sake will receive a hundred times as much and will inherit eternal life."* (Matthew 19:29 NIV)

*"He who has pity on the poor lends to the Lord, and He will pay back what he has given."* (Proverbs 19:17 NKJV)

Remember the rich, young ruler wanted to know how to obtain eternal life, right?

He asked a question, but he didn't wait around for the second part of the answer. Jesus promised eternal life and multiplied increase for all those who are willing to leave what they have behind and follow Him.

---

[21] Luke 4:18

The shackles of lack that bound his heart and mind, are a perfect example of what it means to stop in the middle of class, conscious, society, and self.

In the end, there is nothing in the middle but hollow dreams and empty space. But every man must make the decision to live on top or dwell on the bottom, reigning as the head or being kicked as the tail through his or her own set of thoughtful considerations.

Jesus didn't force the ruler to follow Him. And He won't force you or I either. The place you occupy in life is left solely to your discretion. There is no one to lean on here. Why? Because ultimately, the choice is yours.

You must step to the podium and declare your decision with determined action and soulful sacrifice. There is a daunting question that still remains in the atmosphere of the earth. And all of heaven is waiting to *see* your response.

Will you appropriate your dominion in Christ as a citizen of God's Kingdom in the earth, living to please Him as the head of your life? Or will you exist in the status quo of systematic reliance on other people that never gets you beyond the point of insufficiency, perpetual unproductivity, and fruitfulness?

The solution for every problem that you have is a spiritual one. Jesus Christ demonstrated how to move from the bottom to the top of all things, by staying fully submitted, committed, and dependent on the Father.

Now through His life, you can live another reality. One that is not moved by the futile fluctuations of mankind but is anchored in an unchanging God who extravagantly displayed that no matter where you are, He has made a way upward for you. Whether in the top one percent or the bottom five.

Hopefully, you've come to understand that middle-class living isn't about money at all. And that your station in life stems directly from Who you are connected to. Renewing your mind with God's way of thinking will change everything about you from the inside out including the hope in your heart and the balance of your bank account.

## Clarity and Closure

You now stand at the door of the rest of your life. In this chapter I spoke to you about the potential of you taking dominion over time. You can continue in the time zone of your old way of doing things or you can start your time in life over. No that's not wishful thinking.

*"The steadfast love of the Lord never ceases, His mercies never come to an end, they are new every morning."* (Lamentations 3:22-23 ESV)

*"Therefore, if anyone is in Christ, He is a new creature."* (2 Corinthians 5:17 ESV)

Our great God starts out new every morning, why not just start a new life? Your history has passed away and everything is new. You must be asking the question, 'How can this be?' Well didn't the apostle Paul say in the above verse from 2 Corinthians that "the old has passed away." Simply put are you going to hold on to your old calendar, or why not let it pass away as God's Word says. And move up to God's calendar that starts out new every morning. Before you ask the question, the answer is 'yes'. You can do that according to Job 22:28.

*"Thou shalt decree a thing and it shall be established unto thee, and the Light shall shine upon thy way."*

If you will just accept God's way of keeping time. You can have a new day, an actual start over point to your life, a clean past, to start applying all of the principles of this book. And the Holy Book (the Bible), can by permission of God, wipe away the past and start all over.

*"... but one thing I do, forgetting those things which are behind and reaching forward to those things which are ahead."* (Philippians 3:13 KJV)

There you have from God's own Word a permission slip to move into a whole new life of not just enough into a life of "more than enough".

*"Now unto Him that is able to do exceedingly abundantly above all that we can ask or think according to the power that worketh in us."* (Ephesians 3:20 KJV)

Everything you need is in you. It was placed there when God designed you. Now just start releasing the power of God into your life by applying His way of thinking living, loving, and giving to your life and watch your benefit, the benefit of your family, your church, and those who God points out for you to bless. Don't be afraid. Remember the last words of Job 22:28, *"... and the light shall shine upon thy way."*

God will guide you every step of the way. Be blessed, as God has blessed me in allowing me to share with you the great truths that took me from less than enough to exceedingly abundantly more than I could ask or think.

=The End=

# THE INVITATION

Have you accepted Jesus into your heart? If not, today is your day to change your life forever by accepting the gift of salvation.

**Pray this simple prayer:**

*Father,*
*I thank you for the gift of your Son, Jesus Christ. I denounce satan. I repent of sin. I believe in my heart that Jesus Christ died for me on the cross, was buried and was resurrected from the dead by God the Father.*

*I confess with my mouth that Jesus Christ is the Son of God. I ask Jesus Christ to come into my heart now.*
*Jesus take me as Your own and live in me and through me from this moment forward. Thank You.*
*In Jesus Name, Amen.*

We believe that you have just taken a step that has changed your life forever.

We want to provide you with **Free Resources** to start you on your journey of faith.

Visit us online at **bishopmerrittministries.org** and let us know that you have accepted Jesus as your Lord to receive these resources today.

## ABOUT THE AUTHOR
### BISHOP ANDREW MERRITT

Bishop Andrew Merritt grew up in Detroit, MI with his mother, Laura, and grandmother, Pauline. It was after time spent in Chicago, at the age of 24, that he was called to preach. At that time, he began learning under the ministry of Bishop William Bonner and was ordained in 1972.

In June 1978, Bishop met Viveca Cecelia Johnson in Michigan. The two married on November 4, 1978. Shortly before, on October 28, 1978, they founded the Straight Gate International Church. Services were first held in a storefront building with just three members – Reverend Merritt, his wife, Viveca, and daughter, Rachelle.

Under the powerful preaching and teachings of Bishop Merritt, Straight Gate has experienced phenomenal growth – from three members in 1978 to eight church moves and more than 5,000 members today. Straight Gate is located in the heart of Detroit, still holding true as a family-based ministry, where Jesus makes families whole. The Straight Gate vision is to reach our city, the nation and the world for Jesus Christ. Bishop

Merritt's ministry has touched numerous lives through the local church, radio and television ministries. A man who believes and is best known for his teachings on faith, Bishop firmly believes God has blessed the ministry because of his strong and unmovable faith in God.

Bishop Merritt's dynamic teachings have been published in four books: *Pursue, Overtake and Reclaim,* Jesus *Destroyed the Works of the Devil, The Marriage Enrichment Handbook*, and his bestselling book, *My Faith is Taking Me Someplace.*

"Expectations: I'll Praise," a song featured on Faith in the House (companion CD to *My Faith is Taking Me Someplace*) by Bishop Andrew Merritt and the Straight Gate Mass Choir debuted at number 6 on the Billboard Charts.

As a community leader, Bishop has addressed civic leaders and lawmakers alike. He is one of few African American religious leaders with the honor to have met and participated in various forums with former Presidents Ronald Reagan, William Jefferson Clinton, George W. Bush and Barack Obama. He gave the invocation for the opening session of the Michigan House of Representatives in 1989, as well as, for the October 24, 1990 session of the United States House of Representatives. In 1998, at the request of the Mayor of the City of Detroit, Bishop was one of ten pastors assembled to meet with President Clinton and lead a prayer of healing and restoration for the President and the nation. Bishop Merritt also participated in the first Congressional House-Senate Republican Faith-Based Leadership Summit and was named to the Summit Steering Committee.

Other honors for which Bishop has been recognized include:

**1990:** Minister of the Year by the Michigan Chapter of the Southern Christian Leadership Conference.

**1990:** Co-Chair of the International Mandela Freedom Tour to the City of Detroit.

**1997:** Clergyman of the Year by the Michigan Chapter of the Southern Christian Leadership Conference.

**2003:** Received Key of David and the Keys to the City of Jerusalem and was consecrated as the Apostle and Gatekeeper over the Detroit Metropolitan Region.

Bishop Merritt received a Bachelor's Degree in Theology from the Church of Christ Bible College in New Rochelle, NY, a Master's Degree of Theology from New Covenant Theological Seminary in New York, and an Honorary Doctorate of Ministry from Logos Graduate School in Jacksonville, FL.

Bishop Andrew Merritt was elevated to the office of Bishop on November 24, 1990. His wife, Viveca C. Merritt, and sons Jonathan Merritt and David Merritt share joint responsibility as Pastors of Straight Gate International Church.

Bishop Merritt has six children: Anita, April, Rachelle, Laura (Marc), Jonathan (Tatianna) and David. He is the grandfather of Haki, Kirkland, Mariah, Lorne II, Aaron Andrew, Ryan, Lillian, Josiah, Cristina, Andrew II, and Alexandria.

# Books by Andrew Merritt

- NO Middle Class: Discover a New Way of Living
- My Faith is Taking Me Someplace (***Bestseller***)
- The Marriage Enrichment Handbook: Godly Principles for a Successful Marriage
- Expectation
- Give Your Faith an Assignment
- Jesus Destroyed the Works of the Devil: The Power of a Consecrated Life
- Pursue, Overtake, and Reclaim: A Divine Strategy for Victory
- Promises Don't Die: The Legacy Lives
- Travel Prayers Volume I & II

## Additional Resources by Viveca C. Merritt

- Family Matters: Godly Principles for Everyday Life
- GOD Needs More Annas: A Woman's Guide to Fulfilling Her Purpose
- GOD Needs More Annas: Prayer Journal & Devotional

Available wherever books are sold or by visiting bishopmerritt.org.

@bishopmerritt

www.ingramcontent.com/pod-product-compliance
Lightning Source LLC
Chambersburg PA
CBHW060049100426
42742CB00014B/2756